Layman's Bible Book Commentary:
Micah, Nahum, Habakkuk, Zephaniah,
Haggai, Zechariah, Malachi

LAYMAN'S BIBLE BOOK COMMENTARY

MICAH, NAHUM, HABAKKUK,
ZEPHANIAH, HAGGAI,
ZECHARIAH, MALACHI

VOLUME 14

Page H. Kelley

BROADMAN PRESS
Nashville, Tennessee

4211-84

ISBN: 0-8054-1184-4

Dewey Decimal Classification: 224.9

Subject Headings: BIBLE. O.T. MINOR PROPHETS

Library of Congress Catalog Card Number: 83-26288

Printed in the United States of America

Library of Congress Cataloging in Publication Data

Kelley, Page H., 1924-
  Micah, Nahum, Habakkuk, Zephaniah, Haggai, Zechariah,
Malachi.

  (Layman's Bible book commentary; v. 14)
  1. Bible.   O.T.   Minor Prophets—Commentaries.
I. Title.   II. Series.
BS1560.K39 1984   224'.907   83-26288
ISBN 0-8054-1184-4

To Vernice
my partner and my wife by covenant

Foreword

The *Layman's Bible Book Commentary* in twenty-four volumes
was planned as a practical exposition of the whole Bible for lay
readers and students. It is based on the conviction that the Bible
speaks to every generation of believers but needs occasional rein-
terpretation in the light of changing language and modern experience. Following the guidance of God's Spirit, the believer finds in it
the authoritative word for faith and life.

To meet the needs of lay readers, the *Commentary* is written in a
popular style, and each Bible book is clearly outlined to reveal its
major emphases. Although the writers are competent scholars and
reverent interpreters, they have avoided critical problems and the
use of original languages except where they were essential for
explaining the text. They recognize the variety of literary forms in
the Bible, but they have not followed documentary trails or become
preoccupied with literary concerns. Their primary purpose was to
show what each Bible book meant for its time and what it says to our
own generation.

The Revised Standard Version of the Bible is the basic text of the
Commentary, but writers were free to use other translations to
clarify an occasional passage or sharpen its effect. To provide as
much interpretation as possible in such concise books, the Bible text
was not printed along with the comment.

Of the twenty-four volumes of the *Commentary*, fourteen deal
with Old Testament books and ten with those in the New Testament.
The volumes range in pages from 140 to 168. Four major books in the
Old Testament and five in the New are treated in one volume each.
Others appear in various combinations. Although the allotted space
varies, each Bible book is treated as a whole to reveal its basic
message with some passages getting special attention. Whatever

plan of Bible study the reader may follow, this *Commentary* will be a valuable companion.

Despite the best-seller reputation of the Bible, the average survey of Bible knowledge reveals a good deal of ignorance about it and its primary meaning. Many adult church members seem to think that its study is intended for children and preachers. But some of the newer translations have been making the Bible more readable for all ages. Bible study has branched out from Sunday into other days of the week, and into neighborhoods rather than just in churches. This *Commentary* wants to meet the growing need for insight into all that the Bible has to say about God and his world and about Christ and his fellowship.

BROADMAN PRESS

Contents

MICAH

NAHUM

HABAKKUK

ZEPHANIAH

HAGGAI

ZECHARIAH

MALACHI

MICAH

Introduction

Micah the Man

Micah is generally regarded as an abbreviation of Micaiah, a fairly common name in the Old Testament period (see Judg. 17:1; 1 Kings 22:8; Jer. 36:11). The name means "Who is like Yahweh?"

Micah's father is not identified, which suggests that the prophet was descended from obscure peasant stock. He came from Moresheth-gath (Mic. 1:1,14), an apparent reference to the village of Moresheth in the vicinity of Gath, a onetime Philistine stronghold located in the coastal plains to the southwest of Jerusalem. Elsewhere the prophet is referred to as "Micah of Moresheth" (Jer. 26:18).

During Micah's lifetime, the kings of Judah maintained five fortress cities within a radius of less than six miles of his hometown. They were Soco, Adullam, Mareshah, Lachish, and Azekah (see 2 Chron. 11:5-9). They were built to protect the Judean homeland from attacks from the south. Their presence gave the prophet an insight into what was going on in the land.

Moresheth was not far from Tekoa, the home of Amos, and Micah was like Amos in many respects. Both were fearless opponents of a religion that concentrated on rites and ceremonies but was blind to the rights of the oppressed. Both cast aside personal ambition and refused to be swayed by offers of reward or threats of punishment. Micah expressed his commitment to his task in these memorable words: "But as for me, I am filled with power,/with the Spirit of the Lord,/and with justice and might, to declare to Jacob his transgression/and to Israel his sin" (3:8).

Date

The opening verse places Micah's ministry "in the days of Jotham, Ahaz, and Hezekiah, kings of Judah." These kings reigned from 742

17

to 687 BC. The condemnation of Samaria in 1:5-7 suggests a date for
the beginning of Micah's ministry prior to the destruction of the city
at the hands of Assyria in 722 BC.

According to Jeremiah 26:17-19, Micah was remembered for
having prophesied the destruction of Jerusalem in the days of
Hezekiah. The evidence, therefore, suggests that his ministry
extended roughly from about 735 to 700 BC. This made him a
contemporary of Isaiah, although neither prophet ever mentions the
other.

Background

The eighth century BC brought good times to Israel and Judah.
During the first half of the century, both nations were ruled by able
men, Israel by Jeroboam II (786-746 BC) and Judah by Uzziah
(783-742 BC). Their long reigns ushered in a period of unprece-
dented peace and prosperity.

Jeroboam II restored Israel's borders from the entrance of
Hamath to the Dead Sea (2 Kings 14:25). At the same time, Uzziah
was regaining control over Edom and reopening the port and
industries of Ezion-Geber (2 Kings 14:22). Israel and Judah were at
peace with one another, and together they controlled all the major
trade routes that passed through the Middle East. This gave them
enormous revenues from the caravan trade.

The splendor of the reigns of Jeroboam II and Uzziah was based
on a concentration of wealth in the cities and not on the general
welfare of all the land. Before that time, society in ancient Israel had
been predominantly agricultural. Its transformation into an urban
society brought grave dangers—economic inequalities, class distinctions, indifference to human need, social injustice, corruption in
the courts, and unbridled greed on the part of all the leaders,
religious as well as political.

Uzziah contracted leprosy around 750 BC and was succeeded by
his son Jotham, first as coregent and later as king (see 2 Kings
15:5-7). Jotham's reign also was prosperous, and he distinguished
himself both by his building projects and by his military operations
(see 2 Chron. 27).

Jotham's son, Ahaz, came to the throne in 735 BC and had to deal
with the rising threat of Assyrian imperialism. Assyria, led by
Tiglath-Pileser III, conquered Damascus in 732 BC. Ten years later

Samaria met the same fate, and the people of Israel were taken into exile to Assyria.

These conquests left the people of Judah with a feeling of insecurity. Ahaz proved to be a very weak king and willingly submitted himself to the Assyrians. His son and successor, Hezekiah (715-687 BC), was more assertive and cut himself free from Assyrian control. He also carried out an extensive reform of Judah's religion. According to Jeremiah 26:17-19, this reform was influenced by the preaching of Micah.

Micah, therefore, was active from the relatively peaceful days of Jotham until the stormy days of Hezekiah. He witnessed a double threat to the existence of Israel and Judah. One was the threat from without—the rising power of the Assyrians. The other was the threat from within—the decay and corruption evident in all sectors of society. To the prophet, the second threat was far more serious than the first. Against the greed and covetousness of the rich, the injustices perpetrated upon the poor, and the hypocritical religiosity of the people, he became the protesting voice of an offended God. He was impelled by a burning sympathy for his exploited countrymen and could not remain silent so long as they were hurting.

The Significance of Micah

Micah will always be known as a prophet of social justice. He burned with indignation at the merciless exploitation of the weak by the strong. He saw lust after money as the prevailing sin of rulers, judges, prophets, and priests. Unlike the prophets who tailored their messages to the contributions they received, Micah made the rich the chief target of his attack. In language that was often blunt and unpolished, he summoned them to give an accounting to God for their unbridled greed.

Micah grew up in a rural setting and had a deep distrust of cities, particularly of Jerusalem. He saw it not as "the Holy City" but as "the wicked city," and he became the first prophet to announce its destruction (3:12). He saw no hope for it because it had been built with the very blood of his poor countrymen (3:10). He would have said that any society built upon the exploitation of others has within it the seeds of its own destruction.

Micah's definition of true religion (6:8) is one of his most significant contributions to Old Testament thought. It is surpassed only by that given by Jesus as the summary of the law (Mark 12:29-31). Micah saw the essence of true religion not in ritual acts but in the dedication of the will to God. He expressed in one sentence Amos' demand for justice, Hosea's plea for mercy, and Isaiah's appeal for the quiet faith of the humble walk with God.

Finally, Micah is significant because of his eschatological teachings. His prophecy of universal peace (4:1-4), a hope he shared with Isaiah, is one of the strongest indictments of militarism to be found in the Scriptures. It was also Micah's distinction to receive the revelation that the Messiah would be born in Bethlehem (5:2). This latter passage alone would be sufficient to demand that we give serious attention to his book.

Proclamation of Approaching Judgment
1:1 to 3:12

Title (1:1)

This verse locates Micah in roughly the same period as Isaiah (see Isa. 1:1). The prophet's name means "Who is like Yahweh?" Moresheth lay about twenty miles southwest of Jerusalem. In 1:14 it is referred to as Moresheth-gath, suggesting that it was a small village adjacent to the city of Gath.

Punishment for Israel and Judah (1:2-16)

Micah the countryman denounced the cities of Samaria and Jerusalem and predicted their destruction. His battle cry was, "Down with the cities!"

The Awesome Approach of the Divine Judge (1:2-4)

The Book of Micah depicts the Lord coming forth "from his holy temple" (v. 2) and "from his place" (v. 3). At his appearing, the whole earth trembles. Mountains melt like wax. Valleys split apart with deep crevasses. The meaning of this is that the God who comes to judge his people has at his command all the powers of the universe. All the forces of nature are arrayed against a disobedient people (see Jer. 4:23-26). Micah probably had in mind the destruction caused by volcanic eruptions and earthquakes.

The Doom of Samaria (1:5-7)

Verse 5 suggests that Micah's listeners may have asked "Why?" to all the destruction. The prophet replied that it was all due to the transgression of Israel. The catastrophes were related to the guilt that Israel had incurred.

Samaria had been the capital city of the Northern Kingdom for 150 years. Omri had chosen the site for its beauty and for its natural defenses. He and his son Ahab had cleared away vineyards to build an imposing palace, strong fortifications, and a magnificent city. Micah's message was that because the city had been built up from a harlot's hire—a reference to Baal worship—it would revert to a place for the cultivation of vineyards, just as it had been in the beginning.

Micah's prophecy was fulfilled when Sargon II of Assyria conquered Samaria in 722 BC and took its inhabitants into exile. Sargon's record of these events reads, "I beseiged and conquered Samaria, led away as booty 27,290 inhabitants of it.—I installed over them an officer of mine and imposed upon them the tribute of the former king."[1] The modern visitor to Samaria sees the mountain quite literally covered with orchards and vineyards, planted among the ancient ruins. The site stands as a silent reminder of the inseparable connection between guilt and retribution.

Lament Over the Devastation of Judah (1:8-16)

The prophets did not enjoy preaching judgment to their own nation. At times the burden of such a task became almost more than they could bear (see Jer. 20:7-9). Micah was no exception. The prospects of seeing Judah laid waste like Samaria filled him with anguish and caused him to break out in a bitter lament. Thus he showed that he shared in the suffering that was about to fall on his people.

Words are piled upon words in verse 8 to describe the depth of his grief. His mourning was like that of a person who has experienced a death in his family. His wailing was compared to that of jackals. These animals resemble small wolves, and their sudden howls can still be heard at night in Palestine, filling the air with a sound not unlike that of wailing infants.

Jerusalem is mentioned in verse 9 as "the gate of my people." This meant that Jerusalem was to the land of Judah what a gate was to a walled city. In a time of seige, the issues of victory or defeat were decided at the city gate. Even so, in the approaching conflict the fate of Judah would be settled at Jerusalem. The historical background to this verse may have been Sennacherib's seige of Jerusalem in 701 BC.

Verses 10-16 illustrate Micah's skill at making plays on words. He described an army advancing against Jerusalem from the direction of his own hometown and used the sounds of place-names along the route to describe the resulting panic. For example, verse 10b might be rendered, "Roll yourselves in the dust, you who are at Dustown." Or 13a might be read, "Hitch the horses to the chariots, O inhabitants of Horsetown." It would be as if a prophet should arise today and say, "Richmond will no longer be rich," or "Pittsburgh will become a pit," or "It will be night for Dayton." Moffatt's translation makes a brave attempt to preserve most of these wordplays.

"Tell it not in Gath" (v. 10) had already become proverbial in laments, due to the influence of 2 Samuel 1:20. The other names in the list are those of obscure villages known to the prophet but ignored by the world's historians. None of the world's great lived there; but to the prophet, the men and women of these villages mattered greatly and their suffering was just as real as if they had been well known.

The turmoil in the villages was due to an unnamed conqueror's invasion of the land (v. 15). His coming would cause Israel's "glory" to take refuge in the border town of Adullam. "Glory" probably refers to the king and his officials (see v. 14). Just as David began his career as a fugitive in Adullam (1 Sam. 22:1-2), Judah's last king would end his career by returning to Adullam. The distress David experienced was parallel to the distress about to overtake the ruling king. The circle would be completed and kingship would come to an end.

Micah warned parents to shave the hair of their heads as a sign of mourning for their beloved children, who were going away into

Exile (v. 16). This seems to have been a common custom in the time of Micah (see Isa. 3:24; Amos 8:10). It was prohibited in the law (Deut. 14:1), probably because of its pagan associations. The primitive concept behind this custom was that one's life resided in one's hair and that the offering of one's hair to the dead was like the offering of one's life to them. Such a concept was foreign to the teachings of the Old Testament.

Crimes that Cry Out for Punishment (2:1-13)

It is here that Micah showed himself as the champion and defender of the poor. He rose up to protect those who were being brutally treated and stripped of their ancestral lands. Twice he referred to these victims of oppression as "my people" (vv. 8-9; see also 3:2-3). They were his neighbors in Moresheth and people with whom he was closely identified. By his example, he showed us how we too should stand up for those who are unable to help themselves, who have no political power, and are denied the justice due them.

The Greedy Rich and Their Downfall (2:1-5)

Micah accused the greedy land-grabbers of lying awake at night scheming up ways to take more land from the poor (vv. 1-2). In the time of the prophet, a man's wealth was determined in large part by the amount of land he owned. The rich coveted the small parcels of land held by the poor and sought to add these to their estates. The seriousness of the problem was witnessed to by Isaiah, who condemned those who "join house to house,/who add field to field, until there is no more room,/and you are made to dwell alone/in the midst of the land" (Isa. 5:8).

Elijah had already condemned Ahab's seizure of the vineyard of Naboth (1 Kings 21:1-24). The historian recorded that when Naboth refused to part with his vineyard, this so vexed Ahab that he went home, "lay down on his bed, and turned away his face, and would eat no food" (v. 4).

Who were these persons whom Micah accused of lying awake at night planning how to swindle the poor out of their inheritance? One theory is that they were absentee landlords living in Jerusalem.

A more likely theory is that they were the military commanders and government officials appointed by the king of Judah to serve in the fortress cities located in the vicinity of Moresheth. No less than five of these cities lay within a radius of six miles of Micah's home. They were Soco, Adullum, Mareshah, Lachish, and Azekah, cities established by Rehoboam to secure the access to Jerusalem from the coastal plain (see 2 Chron. 11:5-9). It is thought that these officials used their authority to enrich themselves at the expense of the local people. Micah accused them of hatching their wicked plans at night and then carrying them out as soon as the morning dawned "because it is in the power of their hand" (2:1). They had the power of the state behind them and there was nothing the people could do to defend themselves.

Micah addressed the offenders with the strong word, "Woe!" This was the same Hebrew word—sometimes translated "Alas!"—with which one began a lament for the dead (see 1 Kings 13:30; Amos 5:16). The prophet was saying to these wielders of power, who thought that their futures were secure, that they were actually as good as dead. They were marching in their own funeral procession. This was Micah's way of saying that the wages of sin is death.

The reason their doom was fixed was that, while they had been "devising wickedness" against helpless men and women (v. 1), the Lord had been "devising evil" against them (v. 3). Their plans would be frustrated by God's counterplan.

Their punishment was being tailored to fit their crime. They had coveted fields and taken them (v. 2); now they would lament when these same fields were taken from them and divided up among foreign invaders (v. 4). Their punishment would take the form of slavery and Exile, a form of servitude from which they could not remove their necks (v. 3). They would end up not having any surviving members of their families to participate in future redistributions of the land (v. 5).

Opposition to Micah's Preaching (2:6-11)

The biblical text suggests that Micah was interrupted at this point in his sermon by hecklers who shouted something like, "Don't preach like that! You're trying to mix politics and religion! What right have you to meddle in our affairs? You stick to your preaching, and we'll run the community. Furthermore, we think you talk entirely too much about the judgment and wrath of God. We like a preacher who talks about the love of God. Disgrace will not overtake us, for do not our Scriptures tell us that God's words do good to those who walk uprightly?"

Micah was neither the first nor the last preacher to be told to confine his preaching to people's souls and to steer clear of such "unspiritual" matters as politics, economics, and the problems of society. Those who advise preachers in this manner are usually less concerned about the spirituality of religion than they are about their freedom to do as they please in social, economic, and political matters without ever being rebuked from the pulpit. However, any religion that is worth its salt deals with all of life and doesn't make artificial distinctions between the sacred and the secular.

Micah's reply to those who claimed that God blessed the upright (v. 7) was that they had no right to claim such promises for themselves, for they had risen up like an enemy against the Lord's people (v. 8). The acid test of any person's religion is how he or she treats other persons, especially those who are unable to defend themselves.

The rich and the powerful in Micah's day were oppressing the poor and seizing their property. Even women and young children were victims of their exploitation (v. 9). The exploiters believed in the survival of the slickest and had no pity for those who stood in their way to success.

Micah told the oppressors to prepare to leave the land at once (v. 10). They would be hustled off to Exile, for by their crimes they had forfeited their right to find rest in the land.

Micah concluded his response to those who challenged his right to preach by describing the kind of preacher they would like to hear. First of all, it would have to be one whose sermons had no substance and no basis in fact—one who would "go about and utter wind and lies" (v. 11a). Second, it would have to be one who condoned all of their vices—one who advocated the consumption of wine and strong drink (v. 11b). If they could find a preacher like that, they would call him as their pastor without a moment's hesitation.

Restoration After Exile (2:12-13)

Following the announcement of the expulsion of evildoers from the land (v. 10), the prophet announced the gathering of the scattered remnant of the Lord's people from among the nations. The idea of a small remnant which by its faithfulness serves as the instrument of God's work of salvation appears throughout the Old Testament. No matter how wicked the people of Israel became, there were always those who had not "bowed the knee to Baal" (1 Kings 19:18). They were the Israel within Israel through whom the purposes of God would eventually be realized. God still works through a faithful remnant; if we are not willing to be that remnant, he will choose another.

The picture of the Lord in these verses is that of a Shepherd and Liberator. He gathers his scattered flock, breaks down the walls of their prison, and leads them to freedom. As they march toward their homeland, he goes before them. Freedom comes only from following him. The truth in this for us is that God is always breaching the walls of our prisons and bidding us follow him.

Corruption in High Places (3:1-12)

This chapter spells out the greed of Judah's political and religious leaders and announces the destruction that awaits Jerusalem because of them.

Public Officials Who Behave Like Cannibals (3:1-4)

The prophet spoke to the "heads of Jacob" and to "the rulers of the house of Israel." Since the same group is mentioned in verse 9 and accused in verse 10 of building Zion with blood and Jerusalem with wrong, it must refer to the leaders and public officials in Jerusalem.

The question directed to the leaders of the nation is a basic one: is it not your responsibility to be concerned with justice? The fact that the prophet asked the question indicated that this was the criterion that would be used to measure their performance.

What is justice? The Old Testament concept of justice meant protecting the rights of all individuals in society, regardless of their religious, social, or economic status. In fact, the demand for justice was weighted on the side of the poor, the oppressed, and the helpless members of the community (see Deut. 24:14-15,17-18; Isa. 1:17; Jer. 7:5-7).

Justice in Hebrew thought always had a social orientation. The just man was not merely the religious man or the temperate man or the moral man. Rather, he was the man who defended the cause of the poor, the widow, the orphan, and the stranger. He not only refused to take advantage of another's misfortune but he also raised his voice in protest whenever others did so. He was one who did everything in his power to build a just and lasting society.

We must be no less concerned about the demand for justice in our day. We can no more evade God's question than the leaders of Micah's day. God still asks those in positions of leadership, Is it not your responsibility to be concerned with justice? We must work to change the social structures that rob men and women of their human dignity. We must strive to rid our society of class hatred and prejudice. And we must see that the rights of even the weakest members of society are protected. To do any less is to invite God's repudiation of us and of our leadership.

The leaders of Micah's day not only failed to protect the exploited but also had become the exploiters. Micah did not mince words as he attacked their cannibalistic behavior. He accused them of taking after the poor with meat cleavers, of skinning them alive, of breaking their bones, of chopping them up in pieces, and of eating their flesh. Greed for wealth had changed them into cannibals. This is not a pretty speech, but sometimes plain speech like this is called for lest those who need to be rebuked fail to hear what is being said. We can be sure Micah got their attention!

The mistreatment of the poor was only one side of their sin. The other side was a hypocritical piety. After ignoring the cries of their fellowmen, they cried to the Lord, fully expecting that he would hear them (v. 4). However, they were informed that he would hide his face from them in the time of their distress. Those who do not attend to the cries of others need not be surprised when God fails to hear their cries.

Prophets Who Pander to the Rich (3:5-8)

The prophets were as guilty of fostering injustice as were the political leaders. Their guilt was even greater because more was expected of them. Micah began by describing their sinful behavior (v. 5), after which he announced the punishment that would befall them (vv. 6-7), and concluded with a declaration of his own fitness for and commitment to the prophetic ministry (v. 8).

The prophets were accused of structuring their preaching to correspond to the generosity of their listeners. What came out of their mouths depended on what went in. When fed well, they would preach peace. Cut down on their rations and they would preach holy war (literally, "they sanctify war"). This accommodation of their preaching to the giving patterns of their listeners and to their own self-interests marked them as false prophets. Is it any wonder that they led people astray?

Instead of being obedient to the word of the Lord and proclaiming it without favoritism, the prophets had tried to manipulate it to their own advantage. Because they had turned their eyes and their ears solely to their audience, Micah announced that they would no longer see visions of God or hear words of divine revelation. (vv. 6-7). They would cover their lips in disgrace for they would have nothing more to say. The source of their inspiration would simply dry up. Nothing is so tragic as a prophet without a vision or a messenger without a message.

After announcing a future of darkness and disgrace for the well-fed popularity prophets of Jerusalem, Micah produced his own credentials as a prophet. Instead of having his mouth filled with food, he had his heart filled with power, with the Spirit of the Lord, and with justice and might (v. 8). This divine endowment prepared him to declare to Jacob his transgression and to Israel his sin. Once again Jacob and Israel must refer to the people of Judah and Jerusalem. Micah was ready to face them all, even if it meant standing alone.

What a difference a few persons like Micah can make in a community, persons who are not afraid to get involved, who take the trouble to become informed about the issues, and who have a burning passion for justice. We need persons like that to keep the spirit of justice alive and to make our society more compassionate.

Leaders Whose God Is Gain (3:9-12)

If Micah had one commandment uppermost in mind as he preached, it was the Tenth Commandment, "Thou shall not covet" (KJV). He saw covetousness and the greed for gain as the false gods of the eighth century BC.

This section is directly linked to that which precedes it. Micah, who had been empowered by the Lord to the end that he might expose the transgression of Jacob and the sin of Israel, now gave an example of what that entailed. His opening words, "Hear this," were addressed to these same heads of the house of Jacob and rulers of the house of Israel, that is, to the leaders and public officials stationed in Jerusalem. Their sins, as well as those of the religious leaders in Jerusalem, are detailed in the remainder of the passage.

What charges did Micah make against the leaders? First, that they had abhorred justice and perverted all equity (v. 9). To abhor justice meant to ignore the norms established to protect the rights of the innocent in legal disputes. To pervert equity meant to twist what was straight. Isaiah, Micah's contemporary in Judah, made a similar charge: "Woe to those who call evil good and good evil,/who put darkness for light and light for darkness, who put bitter for sweet and sweet for bitter!" (Isa. 5:20).

The second charge was that the leaders had built Zion with blood and Jerusalem with wrong (v. 10). Micah may have had in mind the exploitation of those conscripted to work on public projects in Jerusalem. They may have been beaten and subjected to unbearable working conditions. On the other hand, he may have been thinking of the money siphoned off from the poor to pay for these projects. The mortar holding the stones together appeared to him to be mixed with the blood of the poor. He was not impressed with the outward splendor of the city. To him it was a splendor purchased at too great a price. This was not the last time that urban renewal has been carried on the backs of the poor.

The third charge is expanded to include not only the civil officials but also the priests and the prophets (v. 11). The charge against all three classes is basically the same: they give their services to the highest bidder. They are all controlled by an inordinate greed for personal gain. These three groups—the judges, the priests, and the prophets—represented the three avenues of appeal open to a person who had suffered wrong. Micah's indictment meant that if such a person did not have money he or she would not even get a hearing from any of these three. What could a poor person do when only money talked?

Micah was not opposed to politicians, priests, and prophets receiving a fair wage for their services. What distressed him was that the love of money had become the overriding concern of their lives and had blinded their eyes to the injustices perpetrated against the innocent. When justice is auctioned off to the highest bidder, it becomes a cruel hoax.

The fourth charge made against the leaders of Jerusalem was that they tried to clothe their greed and cruelty in a cloak of piety. The prophet reported, "Yet they lean upon the Lord and say,/'Is not the Lord in the midst of us?/No evil shall come upon us'" (v. 11). They used the vocabulary of faith but the prophet knew they were faking. They did not have the slightest notion what faith really meant. It was something they had heard about but never experienced.

Micah's "Therefore" (v. 12) came like a thunderclap. To those who regarded themselves as the pillars of society he said, "*Because of you* [the Hebrew is emphatic]/Zion shall be plowed as a field;/Jerusalem shall become a heap of ruins" (author's italics). Those who proclaimed the loudest that the Lord was in their midst were the chief culprits. Those who believed that disaster would never overtake them would see their disaster compounded.

Israel's Travail and Triumph
4:1 to 5:15

Unlike the preceding chapters, this section of the Book of Micah consists almost entirely of words of hope and cheer.

The Exaltation of Zion (4:1-5)

The astonishing thing about this passage is that it follows immediately on the heels of 3:12, which contains an unqualified announcement of Jerusalem's downfall and of the destruction of the house of the Lord on Mount Zion. We go from an announcement of total catastrophe to one of victory and exaltation. We are told that in the latter days Zion will be elevated as the spiritual capital of the world and as the focal point of world peace. It is precisely the "heap of ruins" (3:12) that becomes the most attractive mountain in all the world. What this sequence of passages teaches us is that Zion could only enter the new age by passing through the door of judgment.

The reference to "the latter days" (v. 1) places the expected fulfillment of this passage in the messianic age. The first three verses are found almost verbatim in Isaiah 2:2-4. Various explanations have been suggested: (1) the passage originated with Isaiah and was borrowed by Micah; (2) it originated with Micah and was borrowed by Isaiah; (3) or it did not originate with either but was an anonymous prophecy which was introduced into each of the two books either by the prophets themselves or by another. The evidence is so fragmentary that it is impossible to determine precisely what happened.

The "mountain of the house of the Lord" (v. 1) is to be understood as the Temple mount. It serves a different function in this oracle, however, from that which it served in Micah's day. The nations of the earth come to the Temple not to offer sacrifices on its altar but to receive the law and the word of the Lord (v. 2). The central function of the Temple is, therefore, prophetic rather than priestly. The Law had been given to Israel at Mount Sinai; it would be given to the nations at Mount Zion.

The nations of the earth come not to seek Israel but to seek the God of Israel. Tired of the endless round of war and bloodshed, they are willing for him to become their arbitrator. By their example, they teach us that the way to universal peace and brotherhood is the way of God. We will never get right with one another until we first get right with God.

Of special significance in this passage is the concept that war is a learned behavior (v. 3). This means in the first place that soldiers must be taught the skills of warfare. It also means that the predisposition to war must be instilled in people before they are willing to support a war effort. They must be propagandized. Fear and hatred must be aroused in them, and they must be made to believe that their nation's honor is at stake. When this process has been completed, most nations will fight with a patriotic fervor that generates its own momentum. The illusion is created that being willing to kill and to be killed is a noble thing. After that, it becomes harder to stop a war than it was to start it.

Micah saw a better solution to the world's problems. He saw war not as an inevitable factor in human affairs but as a learned behavior that could be unlearned. The words of this tremendous vision have appropriately been inscribed on the walls of the United Nations building in New York City, keeping before the assembled nations the dream of a world without war. One wonders if we, too, will have to become "a heap of ruins" before we take this dream seriously.

The conclusion to this oracle (v. 4) is missing from Isaiah 2. It asserts that the disarming of the nations will result in the elimination of poverty and fear. This is the Old Testament's way of saying that the only truly effective war on poverty is a war on war. The world will never know prosperity and security until its weapons of destruction have been converted into projects beneficial to humanity. If this is ever to occur, it must be preceded by a universal turning to the Lord such as that envisioned by the prophet.

Micah clearly understood the difficulty of translating his vision into reality. Verse 5 describes how God's people must order their lives in a world that lives with war but dreams of peace. This verse might be paraphrased to read: in the meantime, while the nations walk each in the name of its god, let us walk in the name of the Lord our God for ever and ever. As people walk in the name of the Lord, they are permitting his atoning work to become a reality through their lives.

The Gathering of the Scattered Remnant (4:6-7)

This is a brief oracle of salvation promising the gathering of the scattered remnant of Israel, their transformation into a mighty nation, and the Lord's unending rule over them in Mount Zion. The preceding oracle mentioned the Lord's rule over the nations in Mount Zion but failed to mention Israel. This passage introduces Israel into that future scene. The words that introduce this oracle in verse 6, "In that day," are parallel to those found at the beginning of the previous oracle in verse 1, "in the latter days."

The people of the Lord are described in verse 6 as a flock whose members are lame and scattered. This particular word for lame occurs elsewhere only in Genesis 32:31 and Zephaniah 3:19. A noun derived from the same verb root means "stumbling" or "falling" and shows that a lame person was one who could walk about only with the greatest of difficulty (see Job 18:12; Pss. 35:15; 38:17; Jer. 20:10). Israel was described as a battered and wounded flock, driven out from her homeland, and having experienced the judgment forecast in 3:12. Her future appeared to be grim and hopeless.

At this point, the Lord himself entered the picture and acted to redeem his battered flock. His power and grace overcame their weakness and despair. Micah was fond of showing how the Lord reveals his power through human weakness and transforms that weakness into a tower of strength (5:2; see also Deut. 7:7-8; 1 Cor. 1:26-29; 2 Cor. 12:7-10).

Out of this battered flock, the Lord created a remnant and out of the remnant a mighty nation (v. 7). The same words are used in verse 3 to describe the mighty nations who come seeking the Lord's direction on Mount Zion. Wounded Israel takes her place among the superpowers. She is actually stronger than they, for the Lord is her everlasting king.

The Dominion Restored to Jerusalem (4:8)

The Lord promised not only to gather the bruised and scattered remnant of his flock and to reestablish his rule over them (v. 7) but also to raise Jerusalem to its former position as head over a united kingdom, as it was in the days of David (v. 8). This promise also should be viewed as the sequel to the judgment against the city forecast in 3:12.

The Plan of Men and the Plan of God (4:9 to 5:1)

The division suggested here follows the Hebrew text, which makes 5:1 the concluding verse in chapter 4. The key word in this section is the word "now," which marks the three divisions within the passage (4:9,11; 5:1). A secondary use of "now" also occurs in verse 10.

The "now" sayings reminded Israel of the dark days through which she had to pass before she emerged into the sunlight of God's redemption. After each "now" saying comes a reassurance that redemption is on its way.

The first of the sayings (vv. 9-10) reminded Israel of the agonies of Exile. It would mean the loss of king and counselor and pain like that of a woman in labor. It would mean being uprooted from her land and transported to Babylon, there to languish through long years of servitude. But it would also mean being rescued from there and being redeemed by the Lord from the hand of her enemies.

The second of the sayings relates to the seige of Jerusalem by "many nations" (vv. 11-13). Micah seems to have been the first to speak of an attack on restored Israel by a coalition of hostile nations. This theme reappears in other Old Testament passages (Isa. 17:12-14; 29:5-8; Ezek. 38—39; Zech. 12:1-9; 14:1-3,12-15). The unique feature in Micah is that Israel is summoned to arise and do battle with the nations. In all of the other passages, the Lord himself intervenes to save his people.

The nations are described as gloating over the expected downfall of Jerusalem (v. 11). This would not come about, however, for the Lord had other plans. The assault of the nations was a strategy initiated by him to break their power (v. 12). They had planned one thing, but he had planned another. Those who came to thresh the daughter of Zion would themselves be threshed by her (v. 13).

The command to Zion to arise and thresh the nations contains two qualifying clauses (v. 13). First, Zion was not to act in her own strength but in the strength of the Lord: "for I will make your horn iron/and your hoofs bronze." Second, she was not to seek to enrich herself with the spoils of battle: "you . . ./shall devote their gain to the Lord,/their wealth to the Lord of the whole earth." The verb to "devote" (v. 13) is used of Israel's disposition of the spoils of battle in the stories of the conquest of the land of Canaan (Deut. 2:34; 3:6; Josh. 2:10; 6:18; 1 Sam. 15:3). The holy war concept was carried over here from earlier days.

The last of the "now" sayings (5:1) carries the idea of the seige of Jerusalem a step further. Although there are serious textual problems in this verse and the various translations differ in their rendering of it, the general sense seems to be clear. Jerusalem was laid under seige, and her king suffered humiliation at the hands of the attackers. This may be a reference to the insults heaped upon Hezekiah by Sennacherib's commander during the seige of Jerusalem in 701 BC (Isa. 36:1 to 37:4).

Unlike the first two "now" sayings, the last one does not contain an assurance of deliverance. This is not an oversight, however, for the note of deliverance is sounded in the messianic oracle which follows in 5:2-4. Israel's present king may have been suffering humiliation at the hands of his enemies, but the Lord's purpose was to raise up one from Bethlehem who would rule Israel in glory and in majesty.

The Promised Messiah (5:2-4)

This passage deals with the origin of the expected Messiah and the nature of his kingship. It became one of the key passages in the early church's understanding of the birth of Jesus (see Matt. 2:5-6; John 7:42).

Messiah was expected to be of the dynasty of David and to be born in the ancestral home of David. His birthplace is designated here as "Bethlehem Ephrathah." After the conquest of Canaan, Bethlehem and the surrounding countryside were settled by the Ephrathah clan of the tribe of Judah. This explains why the father of David is referred to in 1 Samuel 17:12 as "an Ephrathite of Bethlehem in Judah." Ephrathah was the name given to the larger district in which Bethlehem was located (see Ruth 4:11; 1 Chron. 4:4), although the two are sometimes mentioned as if they were identical (Gen. 35:19).

The prophet returned to the theme of God's use of things that are weak to confound the strong. Bethlehem is said to be "least among the thousands of Judah" (literal translation). "Thousands" can also mean "fighting unit," "family unit," or "clan." Thus the Revised Standard Version of the Bible renders it, "who are little to be among the clans of Judah." When Gideon was called to deliver Israel from the Midianites, he protested that his "clan" (same Hebrew word) was the weakest in Manasseh (Judg. 6:15).

And yet God intended to take from Bethlehem one who would be ruler in Israel. It was one "whose origin is from of old,/from ancient days." The word for *origin* occurs only here and means literally "whose goings forth." This is probably another word for lineage or family origin. Messiah's lineage was "from of old,/from ancient days." This meant that he was descended from the ancient dynasty of David. He was no imposter to the throne but one whose credentials were valid. The fact that he came from Bethlehem and not from Jerusalem meant that God intended to make a new beginning with the institution of kingship. He called David from Bethlehem (1 Sam. 16); now he called a son of David from the same place. He was taking kingship back to its origins.

Verse 3 indicates that while Israel waited for the Messiah she would continue to be subject to the nations. This verse seems to be an explanation for the delay in the coming of the new king. Israel's time of waiting is compared to that of a woman waiting in labor to give birth to her child. When her time of travail was ended, all her sons would return to her and the stage would be set for the long-awaited ruler to begin his reign.

At the appointed time, he would step forth with divine authority to tend his flock (v. 4). A favorite symbol of the king in the ancient Near East was that of a shepherd. The shepherd's staff was the sign of kingship among the pharaohs of ancient Egypt. The shepherd's care of the flock involved three things: protecting and defending it, feeding and nourishing it, and guiding and directing it. Israel's shepherd would do all of these things in an extraordinary way, for he would do them "in the strength of the Lord,/in the majesty of the name of the Lord his God" (v. 4). The goal of his reign was that his people might dwell secure and that he might be exalted "to the ends of the earth."

Deliverance from the Threat of Assyria (5:5-6)

These verses seem to focus attention once again on the difficult days through which Micah and his fellow countrymen were passing in the eighth century BC. Assyria continued to exert pressure on Judah after first conquering the Northern Kingdom in 722 BC.

Sennacherib laid seige to Jerusalem in 701 BC and boasted that he was able to make Hezekiah a prisoner in Jerusalem, "like a bird in a cage" (*ANET,* p. 288).

According to verse 5, the hard-pressed people took measures to protect themselves from the invader. They raised up shepherds (kings) and princes to oppose him. The numbers "seven" and "eight" must not be interpreted literally. This was the Hebrew way of specifying a large but indefinite number of leaders. Micah was probably thinking of all the leaders who were active in Judah between 722 BC and the end of the century.

Verse 6 confidently affirms that Judah's leaders will conquer Assyria and impose their dominion over it. Assyria is called "the land of Nimrod" because of the tradition that Nimrod was the founder of Babylon and Nineveh (Gen. 10:8-12). Since Judah was never able to conquer Assyria, some have argued that the reference to Assyria is not to be interpreted literally but is to be viewed as a code name for any great power which might threaten Israel in the future. However, there seems to be no compelling reason not to interpret Assyria in a literal sense.

It is difficult to coordinate the description of Judah's leaders ruling over the land of Assyria "with a drawn sword" (v. 6) and that of the nations' beating their swords into plowshares in 4:3. The solution suggested here is that 4:3 refers to the ideal future and 5:5-6 to the painful present of the eighth century BC. Micah lived in a time when some persons in Judah still hoped their nation might over-throw its enemies by force of arms. That hope is expressed in verse 6 but was never realized.

Israel's Influence in the World (5:7-9)

One of the questions which arose out of Micah's preaching concerned the future of those who might survive the judgment which he had announced. Would God cast off his people without mercy, or would there be a future for those who passed through the judgment?

Micah's reply was that, when the nation had been reduced to only a fraction of its former size and only a remnant remained, then God would work with this remnant to make it strong and invincible.

Two figures of speech are used to describe the future of the remnant. They are the dew (v. 7) and the lion (v. 8), alike only in the sense that they are not dependent upon or subject to human control.

The heavy dews that blanket Palestine at night were a source of wonder and amazement to the ancient Hebrews. When God wished to test the knowledge of Job he asked him, "Has the rain a father,/or who has begotten the drops of dew?" (Job 38:28). The Hebrews did not understand that the dew was produced through the condensation of the moist warm air from the Mediterranean. They only knew that it was a gift from God (Gen. 27:28). The giving of it was a sign of his favor (Zech. 8:12), while the withholding of it was a sign of his disfavor (1 Kings 17:1). In any case, human beings had nothing to do with it. They could neither understand it nor control it.

This was why the dew was a fitting symbol of the remnant of Israel. Like the dew and the rain, which "tarry not for men/nor wait for the sons of men" (v. 7), the remnant owed its existence to no one but God alone.

It may be that the prophet also had in mind the life-giving and fruit-producing qualities of the dew. According to this interpretation, the remnant of Israel was scattered among the nations in order that their moral and spiritual influence might be as refreshing and as regenerating as dew is to vegetation. Christians have interpreted this to mean that the church is called to live in the world and to exert its influence among the nations like dew from the Lord.

The second figure of speech, that of the lion (v. 8), represents the remnant of Israel as an invincible adversary of all the nations. Like a lion among defenseless sheep, the remnant tramples the nations, tearing them to pieces, and no one is able to deliver from their hands. From the standpoint of the remnant, this comparison means that the future belongs wholly to them and that no power on earth will be able to overcome them.

Verse 9 should perhaps be translated as a prayer for the success of the remnant: "May your arm be lifted up above your adversaries, and may all your enemies be cut off." Such a prayer for revenge would be inappropriate for Christians to raise against their enemies. Passages like this led some of Jesus' contemporaries to embrace a messianic hope that was ferocious and vengeful. However, Jesus steadfastly refused to shape his ministry by this model.

The Lord's Purification of Israel (5:10-15)

This passage takes us back to the prophet's earlier emphasis upon the judgment of Israel. Just as Micah 4:1-5 is parallel to Isaiah 2:1-5, so Micah 5:10-15 is parallel to Isaiah 2:6-11. This is further evidence that Micah may have been influenced by Isaiah.

Micah condemned all of the things upon which Israel pinned her hopes instead of turning to the Lord. She had to be purged of all these so that her trust could be in the Lord alone.

The verbs used to describe the Lord's purification of his people are especially forceful: "I will cut off" (four times), "destroy" (twice), "throw down," and "root out."

What were the objects of false trust that had to be rooted out? First in the list were the military forces and the fortifications of the land. The horses and chariots, which Micah had probably seen stationed in the fortress cities surrounding Moresheth, were to be cut off and destroyed. The prophets regarded trust in horses and chariots as evidence of a lack of trust in the Lord (see Isa. 31:1).

The use of horses and chariots in warfare was a practice borrowed from the Egyptians in the days of Solomon. Their use represented a great leap forward in the mechanization of war, a wicked use of humanity's inventive ingenuity. Modern development in this same direction has produced fleets of bombers, atomic-powered submarines, and intercontinental ballistics missiles armed with atomic warheads. And each breakthrough in the creation of new weaponry makes the world more vulnerable and less secure than ever before. Will we ever learn the lesson the prophet was trying to teach?

Along with her horses and chariots, Israel's walled cities and strongholds also were to be cut off and thrown down (v. 11). These would have included the fortress cities located near Micah's hometown.

After announcing the destruction of the military forces and fortifications of the land, the prophet turned his attention to the religious practices the people had adopted in their search for self-security. These included sorcery, soothsaying, and idolatry (vv. 12-14). All these things had been forbidden by the Law (see Deut. 18:9-14), but the people of Micah's day had apparently turned back to them.

Micah condemned idolatry because it involved people in the worship of that which their own hands had made (v. 13; see also Deut. 4:28; 2 Kings 22:17; Ps. 135:15-18; Isa. 37:18-19). The temptation to worship the work of our own hands is as real today as it was in the time of the prophet. Our forms of idolatry may be more sophisticated than those that Micah encountered, but they are basically the same. We trust in our own skill and ingenuity to lead us through our problems. We feel more secure trusting the works of our own hands rather than trusting God supremely. And this is what idolatry is all about.

The passage closes with an announcement that the nations will likewise feel the wrath and vengeance of God for their disobedience (v. 15). This meant that Israel's idolatrous neighbors, from whom she had learned much of her wrongdoing, would also be judged.

Judgment and Redemption
6:1 to 7:20

In this third and final division of the Book of Micah, the elements of judgment and redemption are combined. The first part (6:1 to 7:6) deals mainly with judgment, while the second part (7:7-20) treats of redemption and reconciliation.

God's Lawsuit Against Israel (6:1-8)

This is one of the most significant passages in the Old Testament. Its definition of true religion (v. 8) has been called "the Magna Charta of prophetic religion."

The passage is structured according to the familiar "covenant lawsuit" pattern. In such lawsuits, God brought his people to trial for having broken covenant. Examples of this literary form can be found in almost all the pre-Exilic prophets (see Isa. 1:2-9; 3:13-15; Jer. 2:9-13; Hos. 4:1-3).

Covenant lawsuits were designed to restore a breach of covenant and included some or all of the following elements: (a) a call to the witnesses to draw near and to hear the Lord's controversy with his people; (b) an initial statement of the charges against the people; (c) a reminder of past acts of mercy performed by the Lord on their behalf; (d) an elaboration of the charges; and (e) a statement of the punishment to be meted out.

A Summons to the Witnesses (6:1-2)

A threefold summons to hear (vv. 1*a*, 1*b*, 2*a*) is addressed to the mountains, the hills, and the foundations of the earth. In a setting as broad as the world itself, the Lord brought charges against his disobedient people.

The latter part of verse 2, translated in the Revised Standard Version of the Bible, "and he will contend with Israel," would better be translated, "and he will plead with Israel." The verb means to plead or to reason with someone. It is the same verb translated "let us reason together" in Isaiah 1:18. The Lord's appeal to reason shows that he spoke not in anger but in love.

An Appeal to Past Mercies (6:3-5)

The Lord continued to plead with his people, demanding of them, "O my people, what have I done to you? In what have I wearied you?" The prophet did not specify how the people had expressed their weariness. Perhaps they had spoken out against the Lord, as happened in the day of Malachi (see Mal. 2:17; 3:13-15).

When the Lord's question brought no reply from his sullen people, he made an appeal to history. He asked them to remember his saving acts of the past, acts performed not to weary them but to redeem them. Far from causing Israel to complain, those past acts of mercy should have given the people every reason to show gratitude.

The Exodus out of Egypt is mentioned first among God's great acts of mercy. This was the pivotal event in Israel's experience, the event that marked the beginning of her history as a nation. It was an event that was preached by her prophets (see Hos. 11:1; Amos 3:1-2), sung by her poets (see Pss. 77—78; 105—106; 114; 135—136), and commemorated in the best loved of all her feasts, the Feast of the Passover.

God not only led his people out of Egypt but he also gave them leaders in the persons of Moses, Aaron, and Miriam to guide them on their way (v. 4). Furthermore, he caused Balaam to bless the Israelites, in spite of the fact that the king of Moab had summoned him to curse them (v. 5; see Num. 22:1 to 24:25).

The appeal to past mercies ends with a call to Israel to remember what happened "from Shittim to Gilgal" (v. 5). Shittim was the last encampment of the Israelites east of the Jordan (see Josh. 3:1), and Gilgal was their first encampment west of the Jordan (see Josh. 4:19). Between Shittim and Gilgal there occurred the crossing of the Jordan and the entrance into the Promised Land. Israel was to remember all these events in order that she might know the saving acts of the Lord and respond to them in gratitude and in obedience.

A Request for Instruction (6:6-7)

These verses assume that a voice from the audience interrupted the prophet and requested instruction about the kind of sacrifices that were required for sinners to gain access to God. The one requesting guidance is described in individual terms; he spoke in the first person singular and was addressed in verse 8 as "man." Though addressed as an individual, he represented all Israel.

Two things can be said about this person. First, he recognized that he was a sinner and that he needed to be reconciled to God. He spoke of "my transgression" and "the sin of my soul" (v. 7). Second, he assumed that the only path to reconciliation lay through the offering up of sacrifices. He simply wanted the prophet to tell him what kinds of sacrifices would be most effective.

Having asked his question, the speaker himself began to list possible answers. *Should he offer burnt offerings?* These were sacrifices in which the entire animal was consumed by fire upon the altar. *Or would calves a year old be more acceptable?*

What if he offered thousands of rams? He might have been thinking of the extravagant sacrifices of King Solomon (see 1 Kings

3:4; 8:63). *Or would it please the Lord if he offered ten thousand rivers of oil?* After all, olive oil was one of the most precious commodities of life. It lighted lamps, nourished bodies, and had medicinal and cosmetic properties.

The ascending order of extravagance led the inquirer to one final question. *Would he be accepted before the Lord if he offered his first-born son as a sacrifice?* The suggestion was both bold and shocking. Child sacrifice was condemned in the Law (Deut. 12:31), although there were isolated instances of it in Israelite history (Judg. 11:34-40; 2 Kings 16:3; 21:6). The speaker may have had in mind Abraham's willingness to offer up Isaac as a sacrifice (Gen. 22).

The Essence of True Religion (6:8)

Wrong questions elicit wrong answers. The prophet simply ignored the desperate attempt of the questioner to get a ruling on the best kinds of sacrifices. He let him know that his questions missed the heart of the matter. There was a more excellent way to God than the way of sacrifice (see also 1 Sam. 15:22; Isa. 1:10-17; Jer. 7:21-23; Hos. 6:6; Amos 5:21-24).

The inquirer's preoccupation with sacrifice showed that a vital dimension was missing from his religion. He sought through sacrifice to reestablish the vertical relationship, that relationship between himself and God. But he had overlooked the horizontal relationship between himself and his fellowman. His was a one dimensional religion, restricted to the realm of piety. A religion that concerns itself only with the relationship between the worshiper and God is doomed to failure, for one cannot be rightly related to God unless one is also rightly related to one's fellowman.

It was this missing dimension that the prophet sought to supply. He began by reminding the questioner that God had already showed him what his requirements were: "He has showed you, O man, what is good." No new revelation was needed. God had already made his will clear through Moses and the prophets. Most of us don't need a new revelation of God's will as much as we need strength to obey the revelation that we already have.

God's requirements are listed as three, none of which is related to sacrifice. The first is "to do justice." In the context of the prophetic literature, this means setting right what is wrong and protecting the rights of the weak and defenseless members of society (see Isa. 1:17; Jer. 7:5-7; Amos 5:15). It means observing the principle of honesty and fairness in all our dealings with others. When a nation's system of justice breaks down, or when it protects only the rich and allows them to exploit the poor with impunity, that nation is sowing the seeds of its own destruction.

The second requirement is "to love kindness." The Hebrew word is almost untranslatable. It means loyal love or faithfulness to someone to whom we are bound in a covenant relationship. It means fulfilling the obligations inherent in such a relationship even when there are no legal requirements that we do so and no legal sanctions if we do not. Justice is going the first mile; loyal love is going the second mile, doing more than is demanded of us. It is loving someone more than is demanded of us. It is loving someone whose only claim on our love is his or her need to be loved. It means loving someone not because of who *he* or *she* is but because of who *we* are. It is the kind of love God has for us, and for that reason it has sometimes been called "covenant love."

The third requirement of the Lord is "to walk humbly with your God." Its inclusion shows that the vertical relationship has not been forgotten; it is essential that we keep in step with God as we "walk the pilgrim pathway." To walk humbly with God means to walk modestly, attentively, yielding our will to his will and our way to his way.

In our stress on the "humble" walk, we may overlook the significance of the entire phrase "to walk humbly with your God." Only three times in the Old Testament is it said that someone "walked with God." Those exceptional individuals who did so were Enoch (Gen. 5:22,24), Noah (Gen. 6:9), and Levi (Mal. 2:6). This should alert us to the fact that the prophet was speaking of a unique kind of life, a life totally committed to the will of God. It was his way of saying that God seeks not what is yours, but you!

Corruption in the Marketplace (6:9-16)

This passage resembles chapters 2—3 in that it continues the indictment of the inhabitants of Judah and Jerusalem for their sins.

Chief among these are the commercial sins, the sins of unscrupulous merchants out to turn a quick profit.

The indictment is addressed to "the city," the "tribe," and the "assembly of the city" (v. 9). These are probably to be understood as Judah, Jerusalem, and the ruling class in Jerusalem.

This passage follows logically after the first part of the chapter. What the Lord demanded of his people was justice, loyal love, and submission to his will as a way of life (v. 8). What he got from the Israelites was cheating (vv. 10-11), violence and deceit (v. 12), and a style of life patterned after that of Omri and Ahab (v. 16). The outcome would be that all of their labors would lead to nothing but futility and disappointment (vv. 14-15). In the end, they would be mocked and scorned by all the nations (v. 16).

Treasurers of Wickedness (6:9-12)

Ancient Israel had no government agency to set uniform standards of weights and measurements or to see that these were enforced. Exodus 30:13, where mention is made of "the shekel of the sanctuary," seems to have been a step in that direction. The priests apparently kept a shekel of silver (about one-half ounce) in the Temple so that other shekels could be checked by it. However, this seems to have been a voluntary system without force of law. Abuse of weights and measurements seems to have been fairly widespread.

Weights and measurements were often rigged to take away from the customer and to give to the merchant. Amos 8:5 describes merchants who "make the ephah small and the shekel great,/and deal deceitfully with false balances." Micah accused the rich of having accumulated wealth dishonestly through the use of the "scant measure" (v. 10), "wicked scales," and "a bag of deceitful weights" (v. 11).

Such dishonest trade practices are labeled as "violence" (v. 12). The meaning is that whoever robs the poor with a pair of crooked scales is just as guilty as if he had robbed them with a gun.

Some modern equivalents to these ancient practices would be price fixing, improper labeling, and false advertising. They would also include the actions of workers who are content to receive more from their jobs than they contribute or who think nothing of stealing from their companies.

Assets that Become a Liability (6:13-16)

God, who had been a silent observer of the dishonesty, violence, and deceit of the rich, now moved to judge them. The opening words of verse 13 are emphatic and might be translated, "and I on my part." Whoever wrongs the poor must answer to God. Sin against helpless men and women is sin against their Creator.

The punishment of the offenders is expressed in the form of the futility curse. These are judgment sentences which specify an activity and then announce the frustration of that activity. A good example is Amos 5:11b: "You have built houses of hewn stone,/but you shall not dwell in them;/you have planted pleasant vineyards,/ but you shall not drink their wine" (see also Lev. 23:23; Deut. 28:30,38-40; Hos. 4:10; Zeph. 1:13; Hag. 1:6). The main thrust of such sayings is that a breach of the covenant transforms blessings into curses.

The activities that Micah specified were those of eating food, earning money, sowing seed, and treading olives and grapes. All of these were doomed to frustration because of the flagrant crimes of the people. Their assets would become liabilities.

The prophet concluded his charge against the greedy rich by likening their behavior to that of Omri and Ahab (v. 16). This may refer either to efforts on the part of these kings to lead Israel into apostasy and idolatry or to the injustice practiced against Naboth. The latter seems the more likely interpretation. It should be recalled that Ahab, helped by Jezebel his wife, engineered the takeover of Naboth's vineyard and had him murdered in cold blood (1 Kings 21). The unscrupulous men of Micah's day were committing crimes against the poor that were just as despicable.

The prophet pronounced judgment upon the greedy rich in no uncertain terms. Cities would become desolate, their inhabitants would become a "hissing," and they would have to bear the scorn of the nations (v. 16).

Alone, but not Alone (7:1-7)

This passage, cast in the form of a lament, expresses the speaker's disillusionment with the world in which he lived. The speaker is not identified and has been taken to be the prophet or perhaps the city of Jerusalem. It was a world in which every man lived for himself and society was governed by the law of the survival of the slickest.

The Loneliness of the Faithful (7:1-6)

The speaker likened himself to a hungry man going out into a wheat field or a vineyard in order to glean after the reapers. The Old Testament demanded that farmers leave the remnants of their crops in the field for the poor to reap (see Deut. 24:19-22; Ruth 2:1-23). In this instance, however, the fields had been stripped bare. No matter how diligently the speaker searched, he could find nothing worth eating—no grapes, no figs, nothing to satisfy his hunger (v. 1).

This metaphor of the stripped fields was meant to be applied to Judah. Just as nothing worth eating remained in the fields, even so nothing good or worthwhile remained in Judah. The speaker, like Jeremiah a century later (Jer. 5:1-5), was unable to find even one godly person left in the land. The godly and the upright had disappeared, and their places had been taken by murderers and robbers (v. 2). Rulers and judges, who should have maintained justice and order in a time like that, all had their hands held out for bribes (v. 3). Dealing with the best of them was like tangling with briers or running into a thorn hedge (v. 4). Because of the lawlessness and greed in the land, the day of judgment announced by the prophets, the watchmen of Israel, was now close at hand (v. 4). A society that lived by the law of the jungle could not escape the day of judgment.

The sickness had spread even to the private sector of life. The speaker found himself isolated and surrounded by hostility wherever he turned. Not even his neighbor, his close friend, his wife, his son, or his daughter could be trusted. (vv. 5-6). The times were so out of joint that a man's enemies were likely to be those of his own household (v. 6; see also Matt. 10:34-36). It would be difficult to imagine a more depressing situation than that portrayed here. The speaker found himself totally cut off from any caring or sharing community.

Waiting on the Lord (7:7)

Only one avenue of help remained, and that was in the Lord (v. 7). In a ringing affirmation of his faith, the speaker cried out, "But as for me, I will look to the Lord." This verse resembles the confessions of trust which are often found in the laments of the Psalms (see Pss. 13:5-6; 22:22-24; 31:21-22; 130:5-6). A lament which begins "Woe is me!" (v. 1) ends with the words "But as for me" (v. 7).

Three verbs in this verse tell the story of hope regained. "I *will look* to the Lord." This is not the normal Hebrew word for looking or seeing but one which means to watch from a watchtower, or from the top of a city wall (see 1 Sam. 14:16; 2 Sam. 13:34; 2 Kings 9:17; Hab. 2:1). The words for "watchmen" and "watchtower" are derived from this same verb. The speaker was like a man stationed atop a high tower eagerly searching the horizon to see if there was any indication that the Lord was coming to his rescue. "I *will wait* for the God of my salvation." The word used here means to wait in full confidence that one's needs will be met. It means to wait in hope (see Ps. 130:5-7; Lam. 3:21-24). The *Good News Bible* reads, "I will wait confidently for God." "My God *will hear* me." (Italics in this paragraph are authors.) Princes and judges might not defend him, and friends and family might turn against him, but he was sure the Lord was still on his side. There was one forum where his petitions were still heard, and that was the only one that really mattered.

From Darkness to Light (7:8-10)

The theme that runs through the rest of the Book of Micah is that of quiet confidence in the salvation of the Lord. Verses 8-10 constitute the first stanza in this hymn of hope. The voice that spoke in these verses is feminine and has generally been interpreted as the personification of Jerusalem. The city spoke as if she had recently suffered violence at the hands of an enemy. The enemy was also referred to in the Hebrew by the feminine gender and has variously been interpreted as Assyria, Edom, or Babylon.

Ancient peoples believed that a nation's defeat implied that its gods also had been defeated. Jerusalem's foe rejoiced over her downfall (v. 8) and taunted her by asking, "Where is the Lord your God?" (v. 10; see Pss. 42:3,10; 79:10). The question implied that her God was powerless to help her in her distress.

Jerusalem's response was that her foe should not gloat over her.

Though for the moment she had fallen, she would surely rise again. Though darkness had engulfed her, the Lord was her light (v. 8). As God scattered the darkness at creation with his gift of light, even so would he send his light to end her night of suffering and to bring order out of her chaos.

Verse 9 is an admission on the part of Jerusalem that her present troubles were the result of her own sins. Yet she believed that judgment was not God's final word but that his judgment was designed to lead to redemption. After he had chastened her, he would plead her cause, lead her forth to the light, and set her free.

When all this had taken place, the tables would be turned on her enemies who taunted her about the apparent inactivity of her God. The last part of verse 10 is a vivid description of the humiliation that Jerusalem's enemies would endure.

The Restoration of Jerusalem (7:11-13)

This passage either predicts the devastation of Jerusalem or assumes that it has already occurred. Those who take the latter position date the passage, along with the remainder of chapter 7, in the period after the destruction of Jerusalem in 587 BC. There is no indication that Jerusalem's walls were destroyed prior to this.

The purpose of this passage is to respond to Jerusalem's admission of guilt and confession of hope in verses 8-10. The city was told to prepare for the new day which was about to dawn. The announcement was made more emphatic by the threefold use of the word "day," twice in verse 11 and once in verse 12. Each occurrence of the word signaled a change in Jerusalem's situation. First, it would be a day when her walls would be rebuilt. Second, it would be a day when her territorial boundaries would be enlarged. Third, it would be a day when her exiles would return from the fartherest parts of the earth.

The passage closes on a rather grim note. Verse 13 speaks of a devastation which would befall the inhabitants of the rest of the world because of their wickedness. Israel would experience salvation while the rest of the world lay under judgment. We must beware lest we read passages like this with a spirit of complacency.

Prayer and Praise (7:14-20)

Prayer and Response (7:14-15)

The prophetic prayer is that God might shepherd his people with his staff (see Ps. 23:4). They were a people "who dwell alone" (v. 14), a possible reference to Balaam's description of Israel as "a people dwelling alone, and not reckoning itself among the nations!" (Num. 23:9). The prophet also asked God to restore the former territory of Bashan and Gilead to his flock and let them feed there. These provinces, both east of the Jordan, were stripped from Israel by the Assyrians after 734 BC.

God's response is a gracious one. He promised to show his people "wonders," or "marvelous things," such as they had seen in the days when they came out of the land of Egypt (v. 15). The Exodus is regarded throughout the Bible as the greatest demonstration of God's love and power in all of Israel's history.

Praise for the Lord's Deliverance (7:16-17)

The nations that have lorded it over Israel throughout her history would finally be brought to their knees. Their humiliation would mean Israel's exaltation. Their military might, in which they had taken such great pride, would suddenly become a source of shame and embarrassment to them (v. 16). Speechless and unable to hear, they would come crawling out of their strongholds, licking the dust like serpents. They would be made to bow in fear before Yahweh the God of Israel.

Praise for the Lord's Forgiveness (7:18-20)

The Book of Micah ends with a moving confession of faith in the forgiving God. If one searched the Scriptures from beginning to end, it would be difficult to find another passage dealing with forgiveness that measures up to this one.

Seven statements are made to express Israel's faith in the reality of God's forgiveness.

(1) *"Who is a God like thee, pardoning iniquity?"* The verb for *pardoning* means literally "to lift up and to take away." To use an expression that I often heard as a child, it means "to tote." In

Genesis 46:5, for example, it is used of the brothers of Joseph carrying Jacob their father, their little ones, and their wives to Egypt in the wagons that Pharaoh had provided for this purpose. When applied to the forgiveness of sins, it means to remove completely.

"Who is a God like thee?" contains a wordplay on the name Micah, which means "Who is like Yahweh?" Israel's God is an incomparable God, and his uniqueness is nowhere more apparent than in his willingness to forgive (see Ex. 34:6; Num. 14:18; Ps. 103:8; Jonah 4:2).

(2) *"Passing over transgression."* The uses of the verb "to pass over" are varied. Israel "passed over" the Jordan (Josh. 4:22). One could "pass through" a country (Num. 21:22). Or one could "pass by" a field (Prov. 24:30) or a city (Jer. 22:8). To say that God passes over transgression means that he completely ignores it as having any effect upon our relationship with him.

(3) *"He does not retain his anger for ever."* The verb translated "retain" means literally "to grasp with a strong hand," "to seize," "to hold fast." It is used also in Micah 4:9 to refer to the pangs that "seized" the city of Jerusalem. To say that God does not retain his anger means that he loosens his grip on it and lets go of it. To punish is his strange work (Isa. 28:21); to pardon is his delight.

(4) *"He delights in steadfast love."* The verb "to delight" is used of Shechem's love for Dinah (Gen. 34:19) and of Jonathan's friendship for David (1 Sam. 19:2). According to Jeremiah 9:24, the Lord "delights" in kindness, justice, and righteousness. These are the things that are uppermost on God's list of priorities.

Steadfast love means God's commitment to the covenant he had made with his people. It means his unmerited grace which maintained the covenant even when his people were unfaithful. Earlier Micah had exhorted the seekers after God to loyal love (6:8); now he affirmed that God himself delights in loyal love. God's anger may last for a moment, but his love is everlasting (see Ps. 136; Isa. 54:7-8).

(5) *"He will again have compassion upon us."* Compassion has to do with God's attitude toward us as weak, finite human beings. The word for "womb" is closely related to this verb so that to have compassion is to feel toward someone as a mother feels toward the child she carries in her womb or nestles on her breast. It is sometimes also used of a father's pity for his child, as in Psalm 103:13:

"As a father pities his children,/so the Lord pities those who fear him." God's compassion toward us is what gives meaning to our finite existence.

(6) *"He will tread our iniquities under foot."* In the two final statements about forgiveness, emphasis is placed upon God's victory over sin. Sin is poetically described as an enemy whom God must subdue and banish from the earth. The verb used here means "to tread upon," "to trample into the earth." In ancient times, clothes were often trampled upon or beaten out with a stick in the process of being laundered. *The New English Bible,* therefore, translates this statement to read, "[Thou wilt] wash out our guilt." The verb employed in the Hebrew normally refers to the enslavement of people (Neh. 5:5; Jer. 34:11) or to the control of enemies (Num. 32:22; Josh. 18:1; Zech. 9:15). God overcomes sin and sets his people free.

(7) *"Thou will cast all our sins/into the depths of the sea."* The emphasis is once again upon God's victory over sin. Sin is represented as a foe which must be overcome and hurled into the depths of the sea. Just as God cast Pharaoh and his forces into the depths of the sea, so will he dispose of the forces of sin (see Ex. 15:4-5; Neh. 9:11). When this occurs, God's people will be free at last from the tyranny of sin.

Verse 20 anchors Israel's hope for forgiveness and restoration in the promises made to the patriarchs, to Abraham and to Jacob. The prophet believed that God would always keep his promises.

Note

1. *Ancient Near Eastern Texts Relating to the Old Testament,* 2nd edition, James B. Pritchard, ed. (Princeton: Princeton University Press, 1955), pp. 284-285. Hereafter referred to as *ANET.*

NAHUM

Introduction

Prophet

Nothing is known about Nahum except what can be gleaned from the book that bears his name. His name itself means "comfort" or "consolation" (see Isa. 51:3; 52:9).

Nahum's home is given as Elkosh. Its location is uncertain and ancient traditions have identified it with such widely separated places as a village near Nineveh, a village in Galilee, or a village in southwest Judah near the border with Egypt. The latter identification is the one most widely accepted by modern scholars.

Nahum is recognized as one of the most gifted poets ever to write in the Hebrew language. His illustrations are vivid and bold and he wrote with a skill that is perhaps unmatched in all the Old Testament. Poetry is the most difficult literature to translate from one language to another, and Nahum's poetry loses much in translation. It is our loss that we are not able to listen to this prophet speaking in the stately cadence of his native tongue.

Date

The date of Nahum can be determined fairly precisely. The destruction of Thebes, referred to in 3:8-10, was accomplished by the Assyrians under Ashurbanipal in 663 BC. This determines the upper limit for the dating of Nahum.

The predominant theme of the book is the destruction of Nineveh. This took place in 612 BC at the hands of Nabopolassar, king of Babylon. Since the destruction of the city is referred to as still in the future (see 2:13; 3:5-7), it is widely held that Nahum prophesied shortly before 612 BC. If this date is correct, then he was a contemporary of Jeremiah and Habakkuk.

Background and Message

The Assyrians conquered Samaria in 722 BC, and Palestine lay under their domination for the next century or so. They reached the zenith of their power under Esarhaddon (681-669 BC) and Ashurbanipal (669-626 BC). After Ashurbanipal's death, however, decline set in; they began to lose control of their far-flung empire. This set the stage for Josiah's reform of religion in 621 BC, which from a political standpoint was an act of rebellion against Assyria. In 612 BC, Nineveh, the once mighty capital of Assyria, fell to the combined forces of the Medes and the Babylonians. The collapse of that great world capital marked the end of an era.

The prospect of the fall of Nineveh stirred Nahum to action. He spoke out of a deep-seated hatred for the Assyrians. They are called "the guilty" (1:3), the Lord's enemies and adversaries (1:8), plotters of evil and villainy (1:11), vile (1:14), wicked (1:15), the bloody city (3:1), and the harlot (3:4). No one would mourn their destruction (3:7) but instead would find in it cause for celebration and rejoicing (3:19).

Nahum's unmitigated hatred for Nineveh has led to the charge that he was a nationalistic prophet like those to whom Jeremiah was so bitterly opposed. He offered comfort to Judah but never called upon her to repent of her sins. Furthermore, his attitude toward Nineveh stood in marked contrast to that of the author of the Book of Jonah. Was he justified in taking such a hostile attitude toward the Assyrians?

Perhaps the best way to answer that question is to let the records of the Assyrian kings speak for themselves. The Assyrians wrote on clay tablets and vast numbers of these have survived.

Ashurnasirpal II (884-859 BC) told how he treated towns which fell to him in the Lebanon region: "I destroyed them, tore down the walls and burned the towns with fire; I caught the survivors and impaled them on stakes in front of their towns" (ANET, 276).

Shalmaneser III (859-825 BC) spoke of the fate of certain towns that opposed him: "By the ferocious weapons which Ashur, my lord [the god of Assyria], has presented to me, I inflicted a defeat upon them. I slew their warriors with the sword. . . . In the moat of the town I piled them up, I covered the wide plain with the corpses of their fighting men, I dyed the mountains with their blood like red wool" (ANET, 277).

Sennacherib (705-681 BC) told of his attack on Judah and Jerusalem in 701 BC: "As to Hezekiah, the Jew, he did not submit to my yoke, I laid seige to 46 of his strong cities. . . . I drove out of them 200,150 people, young and old, male and female, horses, mules, donkeys, camels, big and small cattle beyond counting, and considered them booty. Himself [Hezekiah] I made a prisoner in Jerusalem, his royal residence, like a bird in a cage" (ANET, 288).

Ashurbanipal (668-626 BC), who may have ruled during Nahum's youth, was one of the most diabolically clever of all of Assyria's kings in devising methods of punishment for his enemies. Concerning certain men who took part in an uprising against him, he wrote: "I tore out the tongues of those whose slanderous mouths had uttered blasphemies against my god Ashur and had plotted against me, his god-fearing prince; I defeated them completely. The others, I smashed alive. . . . I fed their corpses, cut into small pieces, to dogs, pigs, . . . vultures, the birds of the sky and also to the fish of the sea" (ANET, 288).

The same king, describing a campaign against the Arabs, wrote: "I ordered soldiers to stand on guard . . . where there were cisterns or water in the springs, thus refusing them the access to the water supply which alone could keep them alive. I thus made water to be very rare for their lips, and many perished of parching thirst. The others slit open camels, their only means of transportation, drinking blood and filthy water against their thirst" (ANET, 299).

The accounts of such acts of cruelty, selected from a host of others, prove that Nahum's indignation was fully justified. He has fittingly been called the prophet of outraged humanity. Surely, if God is in control of history, he cannot be insensitive to the merciless policies of nations like Assyria. The message of Nahum is that God is neither insensitive nor inactive but rises up to judge all tyrants. Such a message is highly relevant in our war-ravaged world.

The Avenging Wrath of the Lord
1:1 to 2:2

Title (1:1)

The word for "oracle" is often translated "burden." It comes from a verb which means "to lift up" or "to take away." When used of a prophetic utterance, it often designates that which is condemnatory and threatening in nature. It seems to have been preferred as the title to utterances against foreign nations (see Isa. 13:1; 15:1; 17:1; 19:1; 23:1), although it was also used of oracles against Israel and Judah (Mal. 1:1).

Nineveh was situated on the east bank of the Tigris, directly across the river from the site of modern Mosul in Iraq. The walls around the city, the ruins of which can still be seen today, were nearly eight miles in circumference. This was exceptionally large for ancient cities and, according to Jonah 3:3, it took three days to cover the city by foot.

Nahum and Jonah are the only books in the Old Testament to be exclusively concerned with the fate of Nineveh. These are also the only books in the Old Testament to end with questions. The questions serve to point up the vast difference in outlook between the two books. Nahum asked of Nineveh, "For upon whom has not come/your unceasing evil?" (Nah. 3:19). God inquired of Jonah, "And should I not pity Nineveh, that great city, in which there are more than a hundred and twenty thousand persons who do not know their right hand from their left, and also much cattle?" (Jonah 4:11). Nowhere is the diversity of Scripture more evident than in these two books.

A Jealous and Avenging God (1:2-5)

The Book of Nahum has an incomplete alphabetic poem in 1:2-10. An alphabetic poem is one in which the successive lines or verses begin with the letters of the Hebrew alphabet in order. Only about half of the letters of the Hebrew alphabet are used in Nahum's poem and some of these are out of order. This means that the poem either was left incomplete from the beginning or else has suffered in being copied and handed down from generation to generation. Other alphabetic poems occur in Psalms 9; 10; 25; 34; 37; 111; 112; 119; 145; Proverbs 31:10-31; and Lamentations 1; 2; 3; 4.

When the repetitions are taken into consideration, a sixfold declaration about God emerges from verses 2-3a. (1) He is jealous. (2) He is avenging. (3) He is full of wrath. (4) He is long-suffering or slow to anger. (5) He is great in power. (6) He will not clear the guilty. This declaration is similar in form to that found in Exodus 34:6-7, although unlike it in substance. God's avenging wrath, and not his forgiving love, is emphasized in Nahum. There is only a hint of his love in the expression "slow to anger" in verse 3. The message of these verses is that the Lord is a God who is not to be trifled with.

Verses 3b-5 describe God's self-revelation on earth. Here, as elsewhere in the Old Testament (see Isa. 29:6; 66:15; Jer. 4:23-26; 23:19; Zech. 9:14), God's manifestation of himself was accompanied by storms and earthquakes and other strange occurrences in nature. It is as if the elements themselves trembled at his appearing.

His path is in the whirlwind and the storm, and the clouds are but the dust of his feet (v. 3). At his rebuke the sea and all rivers are dried up. Then Bashan, Carmel, and Lebanon all wither (v. 4). Bashan, lying in Transjordan and watered by the snows from Mount Hermon, was famous for its fertility. Carmel was the heavily wooded mountain range that extended across central Palestine and jutted out to the sea near where Haifa now stands. Lebanon, well-watered and famous for its cedar forests, lay further to the north. The withering of these fertile regions is a poetic symbol of God's devastating judgment on Nineveh.

So great is the Lord's power that even the mountains quake before him and the hills melt and dissolve (v. 5). The whole earth is laid waste when he marches forth in judgment.

The Doom of the Lord's Enemies (1:6-11)

Question: Who can stand before his indignation?
Answer: No one!
Question: Who can endure the heat of his anger?
Answer: No one!
With two rhetorical questions, that is, questions with implied answers, the prophet described the inevitable doom of those who opposed the Lord. To his enemies, he was like a consuming fire (v. 6). The pouring out of his anger like fire suggests volcanic activity with hot flowing lava and hails of stones. Fire is often used in the Old Testament as a metaphor of the wrath of the Lord (see Deut. 32:22).

While Nahum stressed the wrath of God toward his enemies, he did not fail to mention God's mercy toward those who trust him. Verse 7 says three things about the Lord's relationship to those who take refuge in him. (1) He is "good." This same thought is expressed in Psalm 34:8: "O taste and see that the Lord is good! Happy is the man who takes refuge in him!" (2) He is "a stronghold in the day of trouble." Psalm 27:1 echoes the same thought: "The Lord is my light and my salvation;/whom shall I fear? The Lord is the stronghold of my life;/of whom shall I be afraid?" (3) He "knows those who take refuge in him." To know includes the idea of caring for and protecting. It also means to be personally acquainted with someone and thus to treat him as a friend.

While the Lord is a stronghold to those who take refuge in him, he is a fearsome adversary to those who oppose him (v. 8). Those who plot against him will feel his avenging blow, but they will feel it only once (v. 9). It will not be necessary for him to strike twice! They will be burned up like bundles of thorns and like dry stubble (v. 10).

As verse 11 is translated in the Revised Standard Version of the Bible, it asks about one who came out from Nineveh and plotted evil against the Lord. Commentators usually interpret this as referring to Sennacherib's invasion of Judah and his seige of Jerusalem in 701 BC. The attitude of his commanders during that seige was marked by arrogant pride and blasphemy against the Lord (see 2 Kings 18:13 to 19:37).

Comfort for Judah (1:12 to 2:2)

Some people in Nahum's day apparently despaired of ever seeing the power of Nineveh broken. The prophet spoke to reassure them. Though Nineveh's forces were strong and numerous, they would soon be cut off and pass away. And with their passing, the affliction that God had brought upon Judah would come to an end (v. 12).

Judah was also comforted by being told that the yoke that Nineveh had laid upon her would be broken and her bonds burst asunder (v. 13). The yoke is often used as the symbol of the enslavement of God's people (see Lev. 27:13). Judah had suffered for over a century under the oppressive yoke of the Assyrians.

Nineveh was again addressed in verse 14. The Lord threatened to do three things to her. (1) He would see that her name was blotted out. (2) He would desecrate her temple by removing the images from it. This was the practice that Nineveh had followed in her conquest of other cities. She desecrated their altars and temples and deported their idols, in signal of the supremacy of her own gods, especially Ashur and Ishtar (see 2 Kings 18:33-35). Now she would experience the punishment she had meted out to others. (3) He would prepare a tomb for her, for she was vile and deserved to die.

In verse 15, the prophet used language reminiscent of Isaiah 52:7 to announce the downfall of Nineveh. He visualized a courier traversing the land of Judah and announcing the good news from the mountaintops. The heart of his message was the word "peace." Peace in Hebrew thought meant more than the mere laying down of arms. Derived from a verb meaning "to be whole" or "to be complete," the word describes a state of wholeness, well-being, or fullness of life. Peace to Nahum meant a rich, harmonious, joyful life in a land freed from the threat of Assyria.

The best way for Judah to celebrate the gift of peace would be through worship. The prophet, therefore, exhorted her to keep her feasts and to fulfill her vows (v. 15b). One of the strongest motives for worship is gratitude and that seems to be the basis of Nahum's call to worship. Judah would be able to worship without fear for she would be assured that the wicked one had been cut off and would never again come against her.

The words of 2:1, addressed to Nineveh, consist of an announcement and four sharp commands. The announcement is that an unnamed conqueror was coming to attack her. The four commands are: (1) that she should position troops on her ramparts; (2) that she should post watchmen to be on the lookout for the enemy; (3) that she should "gird [her] loins," perhaps meaning that she should bolster her courage; and (4) that she should muster every ounce of her strength. The decisive nature of these commands prepares the reader for the battle scene described in verses 3-9.

Verse 2 looks forward to the restoration of Judah and Israel, the Southern and Northern Kingdoms. Commentators generally agree that Jacob represents Judah. These two kingdoms are compared to vines that have been stripped of all fruit by the greedy hands of the Assyrians.

The Fall of Nineveh
2:3-13

The rest of the Book of Nahum is devoted to an account of the destruction of Nineveh. Two poems chronicle that destruction with a series of vivid impressionistic pictures (2:3-13; 3:1-19).

The Assault on the City (2:3-9)

Nahum had an eye for color. He described the red shields, perhaps made of dyed leather (see Ex. 25:5), and the scarlet battle dress of the soldiers attacking Nineveh (v. 3). He also took note of the polished metal of their chariots, which made them appear to be on fire as they reflected the rays of the sun. As they raced through the streets of the city, they flashed like bolts of lightning (v. 4).

The "officers" mentioned in verse 5 could be those of the forces attacking Nineveh or those of the forces defending the city. The former seems to be the more likely possibility. According to this interpretation, the verse pictures the lightning advance of the troops, their arrival at the city walls, and the setting up of their military equipment. The "mantelet" means literally the "covering" or "booth." Its exact nature is not known, but it was probably some sort of screen that shielded those who manned the battering rams from missiles thrown down from above.

Part of the attack on the city involved the opening of what are called "the gates of the rivers" (v. 6, KJV). As a result, the palace is said to be "in dismay", or "deluged" (Jewish Publication Society translation), or "topples down" (NEB). It isn't clear what the expression, "the gates of the rivers" (KJV), refers to. Since the city was encircled by the Tigris River and other smaller streams, and since the city was protected by a deep moat around the outer defense walls, some have interpreted this as a reference to the sluice gates that controlled the water level in the moat. When the gates were opened, the moat could be drained, thus making the city more vulnerable to attack. An alternate view is that these were floodgates located in dams upstream from the city. According to this view the invaders opened the floodgates, causing the city to be flooded and the foundations of the palace to be undermined. Diodorus, an ancient Greek historian, records that the river rose from a series of heavy downpours and that this contributed to the downfall of the city.

The queen, referred to in verse 7 as Nineveh's "mistress," is stripped naked and carried off, while her maidens moan and beat upon their breasts.

The comparison of the city to "a pool/whose waters run away" (v. 8) has sometimes been interpreted as a figure of the fleeing population. Although the officers cry, "Halt! Halt!" no one turns back. Another interpretation is that the city is flooded and that the swirling waters will not heed the command to turn back. The first of these interpretations is preferred by most commentators.

Verse 9 is a summons from the prophet to the conquerors, telling them to plunder the endless treasures of silver and gold laid up in Nineveh. The Assyrians had made war their chief national industry, and they had grown rich on the plunder of many nations. Now they themselves were to experience what it was like to be plundered.

The Plundering of the Lions' Den (2:10-13)

The Assyrian rulers made the lion the symbol of their kingdom. They filled Nineveh with statues of lions, for as the lion lorded it over the beasts of the earth, so they thought of themselves as lording it over the kingdoms of the earth.

Nahum took up this theme and likened Nineveh to a lions' den and a cave where the young lions lived. From here the older lions had gone forth in search of prey to feed the lionesses and the young cubs (v. 11). Nineveh's lionesses and cubs had always been well fed, for their cave was filled with the torn flesh of victims (v. 12).

But now the situation had been reversed. The lions' den had been plundered, and the young lions had been slain by the sword (v. 13). No longer was prey brought to the den. No longer did the king's messengers go forth to collect tribute. The reason was that the Lord himself had risen up as Nineveh's adversary.

The triumph of Nineveh's enemies struck terror in the hearts of its inhabitants. Verse 10 describes their consternation. The first three words in the verse—translated in the Revised Standard Version of the Bible to read "Desolate! Desolation and ruin!"—sound almost identical in Hebrew. It is difficult to reproduce this effect in translation, although some translators have attempted to do so. *The New English Bible* reads: "Plundered, pillaged, stripped bare!" The *Good News Bible* reads: "Nineveh is destroyed, deserted, desolate!" The remainder of the verse describes a city in a state of panic. This is a far cry from the days when Nineveh ruled the world.

Lament Over a Doomed City
3:1-19

The theme of this chapter is that no nation is immune to God's judgment if it lives by the power of the sword and follows a policy of ruthlessness toward other nations. Assyria's history was one of uninterrupted ruthlessness from beginning to end. Nahum's satisfaction over the fall of such a cruel and wicked nation was shared by other prophets. For example, Zephaniah wrote: "And he will stretch out his hand against the north,/and destroy Assyria; and he will make Nineveh a desolation,/a dry waste like the desert. . . . This is the exultant city that dwelt secure, that said to herself,/'I am and there is none else.' What a desolation she has become,/a lair for wild beasts! Every one who passes by her/hisses and shakes his fist" (Zeph. 2:13,15).

The Sights and Sounds of War (3:1-3)

Nahum's poetic genius is especially evident in these verses. He delivered a vivid and staccato-like description of the attack upon Nineveh.

The passage begins with "Woe," and what follows is a taunt song over the city's downfall. Nineveh is called "the bloody city," or literally "the city of bloods." When "bloods" occurs in its plural form, it denotes blood that has been shed through acts of murder and violence (see Gen. 4:10; 2 Sam. 3:28; 16:7-8; 2 Kings 9:26; Isa. 1:15; Ezek. 22:2; Hos. 4:2; Mic. 3:10). A good paraphrase of the words of Nahum 3:1 would be "the murderous city." Violence is here linked to lies or deceit, as also in Psalms 5:6 and 55:23. The meaning of the verse is that Nineveh's wealth has been acquired through violence and lies.

As we read verses 2 and 3, we can hear the cracking of whips and the clashing of swords. We also can see the dust of battle, the galloping horses, the bounding chariots, the flashing swords, the glittering spears, and the growing heaps of the dead and dying. Only those who have known the horrors of war can fully appreciate a passage like this. It seems obvious that the prophet himself had witnessed the sights and sounds of war and was writing out of his own experience.

A Harlot in Distress (3:4-7)

This section serves to justify the severity of the punishment that was about to fall upon Nineveh. She was likened to a brazen harlot who had seduced the nations through her deadly charms. "Charms" probably has reference to the superstitions and sorceries that are so widely attested in Assyrian literature. Astrology was commonly used in Assyria in foretelling the future. Omens were sought in dreams, the shapes of animal livers, the formations of clouds, the casting of lots, and the configurations made by pouring oil on water. Sickness and disease were attributed to evil spirits, and elaborate ceremonies were designed to placate these. Ashur, the patron god of Nineveh, was cruel and warlike, and the people took this as an indication that they were to be the same. A nation always becomes like that which it worships.

God himself entered the fray against Nineveh (vv. 5-6). He punished her for the harlot that she was. God is represented as disgracing Assyria with the punishment that was normally meted out to harlots (see Isa. 47:3; Jer. 13:22,26; Ezek. 16:37; Hos. 2:10). Acting almost as if he were the wronged husband, he lifted the skirts of Nineveh above her head (literally, "up to your face") and allowed the nations to gaze on her naked body. He even cast filth on her, thus bringing her into contempt and causing her to become a gazing stock. Many modern interpreters have found such language to be distasteful and have tried to tone it down. It must never be forgotten, however, that God is the active opponent of every nation, no matter how rich and powerful it may be, that spurns his rule and tramples upon human rights. The metaphors used here are not too strong to describe the fate of all such nations.

Nineveh dropped out of history to no one's regret because her cruelties had alienated her from all other nations (v. 7; see Isa. 10:12-19; Ezek. 32:22-23). The prophet's question, "Whence shall I seek comforters for her?" is rhetorical in nature and expects the answer to be, "Nowhere!"

The Example of Thebes (3:8-11)

The prophet demanded of Nineveh if she thought she were better than Thebes. The real point of the question is whether the defenses of Nineveh were better than those of Thebes. The comparison was appropriate, for the two cities were alike in many ways. Both were capital cities. Thebes, the capital of upper Egypt, lay about four hundred miles south of Cairo. Both were located on rivers, Nineveh on the Tigris and Thebes on the east bank of the Nile. Both considered themselves to be impregnable.

And yet Thebes was conquered about 661 BC by an Assyrian ruler! Ashurbanipal told how he captured this Egyptian stronghold: "From Thebes I carried away booty, heavy and beyond counting: silver, gold, precious stones, his entire personal possessions, linen garments with multicolored trimmings, fine horses, certain inhabitants, male and female. . . . Thus I carried off from Thebes heavy booty, beyond counting. I made Egypt and Nubia feel my weapons bitterly and celebrate my triumph" (ANET, p. 295).

Although Thebes was situated by the Nile—here called "sea"—and although it was allied with Put (Ethiopia) and the Libyans, it still did not escape the sword. Therefore, why should Nineveh, whose defenses are much less formidable than those of Thebes and who had no staunch allies, possibly hope to escape? The prophet described the city's fate as that of a person in a drunken stupor, too dazed to defend himself and concerned only with finding a way of escape (v. 11).

Futile Efforts at Defense (3:12-18)

Far from being stronger than Thebes, Nineveh's protecting fortresses were like ripe figs ready to fall into the mouth of anyone who shook the fig tree (v. 12). Her defenders were no better than women, lacking in courage and unable to defend themselves (v. 13). To accuse soldiers of being like women was about the worst insult that could be hurled at them in the Old Testament period (see Isa. 19:16; Jer. 50:37; 51:30). Modern preachers would be wise to choose a different metaphor!

Nineveh's position was actually so precarious that the prophet could speak of her gates as being wide open to her foes (v. 13). Fire had already devoured the bars that secured the gates. She could be had for the taking.

In a tone of derision, the prophet called upon the city to prepare for her defense. She was to draw water for the seige (v. 14). This was of primary importance because one of the first actions of an invading army would be to cut the city's water supply. She was to also strengthen her fortresses, manufacturing clay bricks to be used for this purpose (v. 14).

That the prophet was speaking in derision is clear from verse 15. All of Nineveh's efforts to achieve military preparedness would not prevent her destruction by fire and sword. There is no armament program that can provide lasting security for a nation that has forfeited its moral right to exist.

Nineveh could not trust in her large population to save her. Though her inhabitants were many and though her merchants, princes, and scribes were as numerous as grasshoppers (v. 15) and stars (v. 16), they would all leave her in her time of distress. All her helpers were compared to swarms of locusts and grasshoppers. They settle on the fence hedges on a cold day; but when the sun warms them, they fly away, and no one knows where they are (v. 17).

Actually, the fate of Nineveh's ruling classes, her shepherds and nobles, would be far worse. They would sleep the sleep of death with no one to arouse them (v. 18). Having no shepherd to tend them, the people of the city would be scattered like lost sheep upon the mountains, with none to gather them (v. 18).

Jubilation Over a Tyrant's Downfall (3:19)

The concluding verse in Nahum's prophecy is like a requiem for a dead city. Nineveh lived in splendor but she died in dishonor. Instead of mourning her death, all who heard the news clapped their hands in joy.

The Book of Nahum closes with a rhetorical question, in this instance one that expects a negative answer.

Question: "For upon whom has not come/your unceasing evil?"

Answer: "No one!"

The destruction of Nineveh was unique in many ways. Other ancient cities were destroyed but later rebuilt. Nineveh was destroyed but never rebuilt—not even to this day.

HABAKKUK

Introduction

The Prophet

The name Habakkuk occurs only twice in this book (1:1; 3:1) and is found nowhere else in the Old Testament. Its form is unusual for Hebrew names and its meaning is uncertain. Ancient Jewish rabbis associated it with a verb meaning "to embrace." Because of this association, a legend grew up that he was the son of the Shunamite woman mentioned in 2 Kings 4:8-17 since she was promised that she would "embrace a son" (v. 16).

This legendary story is matched by still another in the apocryphal book *Bel and the Dragon* (33-39). The second story recounts that Habakkuk once prepared a bowl of pottage to take to the reapers in his field. On his way to the field, an angel stopped him and told him to take the pottage to Daniel in Babylon, for he had been thrown into the lions' den. When Habakkuk protested that he did not know the way, the angel lifted him up by the hair of his head and took him to Babylon. When Daniel saw him, he thanked God for remembering him and then arose and ate the pottage. Habakkuk was again lifted up by his hair and transported back to the land of Judah.

The beginning of this apocryphal story states that Habakkuk was the son of a man named Joshua, who was of the tribe of Levi. Scholars have suggested that the tradition that Habakkuk was a Levite may indeed be true, although the story of his visit to Daniel is not to be taken seriously. The Levites were leaders in the Temple worship in Jerusalem, and chapter 3 of Habakkuk certainly has the character of a hymn designed for Temple use. It was not unusual for prophets to come from priestly families, as was the case with both Jeremiah and Ezekiel.

Date and Background

The Book of Habakkuk was written against the background of the early campaigns of the Chaldeans (another name for the Babylonians) against Judah (see Hab. 1:6). Most commentators favor a date around 600 BC.

The Chaldeans seized control of Palestine from the Egyptians at the Battle of Carchemish in 605 BC. They promptly demanded of Jehoiakim, king of Judah (608-597 BC), that he swear allegiance to them and pay an annual tribute. They likely would have permitted him to remain in power had he not rebelled against them around 600 BC. This move led Nebuchadnezzar, king of the Chaldeans, to marshal his forces and to march against the land. Jehoiakim's rebellion proved to be very costly. Judah's cities were devastated, her territory divided, her economy crippled, and her leading citizens exiled to Babylon (2 Kings 24:10-17). Her humiliation was exceeded only by that which she experienced some ten years later in the final destruction of Jerusalem and the exile of the rest of her citizens.

The Babylonian invasion of Judah shortly after 600 BC gave rise to a theological crisis fully as acute as the military crisis. Where was God in all this? Some of the contemporaries of Habakkuk began to suspect that God had lost control over events to more powerful gods. Some even decided to play it safe and offer sacrifices to those other gods (see Jer. 7:17-19; 44:15-19; Ezek. 8:1-18). Others, while resisting outright apostasy, were nevertheless driven to doubt God's goodness and his justice (see Jer. 31:29; Ezek. 18:2,25). What was needed at this time was a reaffirmation of the Lord's sovereign power and of his justice.

It is no accident, therefore, that this is the major theme of Habakkuk. He probably delivered his message in the latter part of Jehoiakim's reign, just before the Babylonian invasion. He saw the Babylonians as the instruments of the Lord's chastening of his rebellious people (1:2-11). However, he believed that once they had served the purpose ordained for them they also would be judged (2:4-17). He was also confident that the Lord, who ruled from everlasting (1:12), was uncompromising in his opposition to evil (1:13). He alone was God, and he shared his rule with no other (2:18-20). It behooved his people, therefore, to wait for him in trust (2:4) and to rejoice in the hope of his salvation even when outward circumstances militated against this (3:16-19).

Habakkuk's Influence on Later Generations

Habakkuk exerted a powerful influence on later Jewish and Christian thought. In the two centuries before Christ and continuing until about AD 70, a band of pious Jews settled at Qumran on the northwestern shores of the Dead Sea. They were an oppressed group seeking refuge from the priestly hierarchy in Jerusalem. Much of their time was spent studying and copying Old Testament Scriptures and other religious texts. There is evidence that the Book of Habakkuk held a special fascination for them. The evidence lies in an unusual verse-by-verse commentary which they prepared on the first two chapters of the book. They saw a close parallel between the hard time Judah encountered around 600 BC and the difficulties that drove them to seek refuge in the desert. They identified the evildoers mentioned in Habakkuk as those who were persecuting them. From the prophet, they received encouragement to wait patiently for the Lord, no matter how long their troubles might last. Thus they took Habakkuk's problem to be their problem and his solution to be their solution. No other prophet had a greater influence upon their life-style and theology than he.

Habakkuk's influence on Christian thought came primarily through the apostle Paul. When Paul was engaged in bitter controversy with the Judaizers, Habakkuk 2:4b—"The righteous shall live by his faith"—became the scriptural weapon he used against them. This text became the cornerstone of his doctrine of salvation (see Rom. 1:17; 3:21-22; Gal. 3:11; Phil. 3:9). By it he understood that justification was by grace through faith alone and in no way dependent upon the works of the law.

Habakkuk's influence spread even further when Martin Luther discovered Paul's doctrine of justification by faith and that discovery gave birth to the Protestant Reformation. There is a real sense in which all Protestants and Evangelical Christians are the spiritual heirs of this Old Testament prophet.

No review of Habakkuk's influence would be complete without mentioning the multitude of persons across the centuries who in the face of suffering, abuse, and spiritual perplexity have drawn strength from his book. Wherever the book has been read or proclaimed, bewildered men and women have been helped by its triumphant affirmation that the righteous shall live by faith. They have drawn courage from its promise that "the earth will be filled/with the knowledge of the glory of the Lord,/as the waters cover the sea" (2:14). And they have learned from the prophet that the Lord's salvation will surely come and that they must wait patiently for it, even though it tarry long (2:3; 3:17-19). This is a book to which all may turn who wrestle with doubts and perplexities and who reject easy solutions to complex problems.

Conversations Between Habakkuk and God
1:1 to 2:5

Title (1:1)

The Bible tells us nothing about Habakkuk other than what is recorded here and in 3:1. In both passages, he is referred to simply as "the prophet." Some have connected his name with a verb meaning "to embrace." Others see a possible relationship between it and the Assyrian word *hambakuku*, which was not only the name of a garden plant but was also a proper name.

The musical notation at the end of the book may indicate that the prophet was a member of the Temple choir, hence a Levite (see 1 Chron. 23:2-6; see the Introduction for other evidence of his being a Levite).

All we know for certain is that Habakkuk was a prophet and that he lived at a time when the Chaldeans were threatening Judah (1:6). His ministry is usually dated around 600 BC, when Jehoiakim's rebellion provoked an attack by Nebuchadnezzar on the land of Judah (see 2 Kings 24:1-5).

Habakkuk's First Complaint (1:2-4)

Habakkuk spoke in the familiar language of the lament as he questioned God about the deplorable moral and spiritual decay in

Judah. His complaint seems to reflect the latter part of Jehoiakim's reign, when social and religious abuses were widespread (see Jer. 22:13-17). Thus, while the major portion of the book deals with the sins of Babylon and the judgment in store for her, attention is also given to the sins of Judah. The prophet deplored injustice and violence wherever they were found, whether in Judah or in Babylon.

The language of lament is especially evident in the opening cry of verse 2—"O Lord, how long?" We are familiar with this cry in the psalms of lament (see Pss. 13:1-2; 74:10-11; 79:5; 89:46). The prophet was not asking for a timetable. He was not asking whether he was under a one-year or two-year contract to prophesy. Rather, Habakkuk was uttering a cry of being neglected, a desperate appeal for God's intervention in a world which he felt God had abandoned. We might paraphrase his cry, "How eternally long, O Lord, will you permit violence and destruction to go on unchecked? How long will you remain silent while the righteous suffer and the wicked prosper and thrive?"

The law, without which there could be no order or justice in society, had grown slack (v. 4). A more literal translation is that it had grown "cold" or "numb." It had become lifeless and inoperative in the restraint of injustice. As an influence in the lives of the people, it was null and void. The prophet probably had reference to the law of Deuteronomy, which had been discovered in the Temple some twenty years earlier during the reign of Josiah (2 Kings 22:8-13). This seems to be an indication that by 600 BC the gains of Josiah's reform had been lost and daily life in Judah had ceased to be regulated by the law of the Lord. As a result, the wicked surrounded the righteous and justice was perverted (v. 4b). This means that the wicked encircled the righteous so that they had no way of escape (see Job 3:23). Justice had been eliminated from society or else existed only in perverted forms.

God's Response (1:5-11)

God answered Habakkuk's complaint by telling him to look out across the nations and see the amazing thing he was about to do. The extraordinary nature of his action is indicated by the string of imperatives—"Look . . . see; wonder and be astounded." God's work was so unusual that one would have to see it to believe it (v. 5; see also Isa. 52:14 to 53:1).

God was about to punish the land of Judah by the hand of the Chaldeans (Babylonians), that fierce and powerful nation before whom none could stand (v. 6). Verse after verse in this passage describes their fierceness. They are called "that bitter and hasty nation" (v. 6). Their presence inspired dread and terror (v. 7). Their horses were swift and fierce (v. 8). They invaded lands only to do violence to them and to take their peoples into captivity (v. 8). No fortress was strong enough to withstand their assaults (v. 9). They were totally irresistible, a nation of guilty men, who worshiped at the altar of military might (v. 11).

There was no indication in God's response that he would separate the righteous and the wicked and allow the Chaldeans to chastise the wicked only. Instead, the clear intent of his words was that the invaders would run roughshod over the entire land, terrorizing the innocent and the guilty alike. The characterization of their deeds as deeds of "violence" (v. 9) draws upon the very same word that the prophet had earlier used in his complaint against conditions in Judah (vv. 2-3). There was nothing, therefore, in God's response to give assurance or comfort to the prophet. It only served to make the mystery of God's involvement in history even more perplexing.

Habakkuk's Second Complaint (1:12-17)

The prophet was taken completely by surprise when the Lord announced that he was using the Chaldeans as instruments of his judgment against Judah and the nations. How could this be? How could the Lord permit such a godless nation to grind the little people of the earth under its heels and do nothing to deter it? How could he allow the wicked to swallow up the righteous and not intervene? The Chaldeans were catching men in their nets like fish. They even made idols of their instruments of war offering sacrifices to their nets and burning incense to their seines. It was absurd that God should allow them to go on filling their nets and mercilessly slaying the nations. Why did he not do something to bring a halt to this senseless slaughter? The prophet had complained to God of violence and oppression, but the answer he received in return only seemed to promise more of the same.

One thing that this says to us is that God does not allow his deeds and purposes to be controlled by persons, not even by righteous persons. He is and remains the sovereign Lord, always free to act unhindered, whether in judgment or in mercy.

But the passage also suggests that it is all right for us to return to God when we are not satisfied with the answers he gives to life's dark mysteries. Sometimes we feel like the woman who had lost her husband in a tragic accident. She sought out the hospital chaplain and asked him if there were a place where she might go and scream. He replied that he would take her to the chapel where she might pray. "But you don't understand," she protested. "I don't feel like praying. I just want to scream." Sometimes all we feel like doing is screaming, and I am convinced that a loving God hears us even when we scream.

Donald E. Gowan has suggested that there ought to be a place in our worship services for such cries as burst forth from the lips of Habakkuk. He writes, "Should there be a place in public, Christian worship for liturgies such as those in Habakkuk and the psalms of lament? Christian worship tends to be all triumph, all good news (even the confession of sin is not a very awesome experience because we know the assurance of pardon is coming; it's printed in the bulletin). And what does that say to those who, at the moment, know nothing of triumph? That they've muffed it, somehow? That their faith hasn't been strong enough to grant them success? That the whole business is a fraud?"[1]

When the prophet accused the Chaldeans of sacrificing to their net and burning incense to their seine (v. 16), he showed a familiarity with their religious practices. The chief gods of Babylon, such as Marduk, Adad, and Ishtar, were gods of war and were given credit for Babylon's victories and conquests. According to Ezra 1:7, when Nebuchadnezzar conquered Jerusalem he removed the treasures from the Temple and placed them in the house of his gods. This is the kind of action Habakkuk had in mind when he accused Nebuchadnezzar of sacrificing to his net and burning incense to his seine. This means that he paid homage to the gods of war who enabled him to conquer nations and to live in luxury.

A Vision for the Waiting Prophet (2:1-5)

After uttering his complaint, the prophet stood like a watchman upon his tower, awaiting the Lord's response (2:1). The language of this verse says two things about Habakkuk. First of all, it underscores his patience and persistence in seeking a word from the Lord. Like a lonely sentinel stationed upon a watchtower, he surveyed the landscape and searched the distant horizon to see if there were any revelation from the Lord. To wait for the Lord is sometimes the hardest part of praying, but it can also be the most rewarding (see Mic. 7:7; Isa. 40:31).

In the second place, Habakkuk's waiting was a recognition of the Lord's sovereignty and freedom. God could not be coerced or cajoled into speaking. Even so faithful and dedicated a prophet as Jeremiah once had to wait several days for a word from the Lord (Jer. 28:10-14) and on still another occasion had to wait for his prayer to be answered (Jer. 42:4-7). Habakkuk could only be prepared to receive the word of the Lord when it came; there was no way he could command it.

As the prophet awaited a word from the Lord, he was told what to do with it when it came. He was to write it plainly upon tablets (v. 2a). The verb translated "make it plain" occurs elsewhere only in Deuteronomy 1:5 and 27:8. Its first occurrence has to do with Moses' explaining the law to the people of Israel. The second passage provides a close parallel to Habakkuk 2:2. In it Joshua was told that, when he had crossed the Jordan, he was to set up stones on Mount Ebal, covering them with plaster, and writing on them "all the words of this law very plainly" (Deut. 28:4-7). It should be noted that both Joshua and Habakkuk were commanded to write down the word of the Lord. Each was also instructed to write the word plainly so that it could be read and understood. Joshua wrote upon stone, while Habakkuk wrote upon clay tablets. The word for *tablet* is perhaps borrowed from the Akkadian language, where it designated a sun-baked tablet written in the cuneiform script. Such tablets were so durable that hundreds have survived and have been dug up and translated by modern archaeologists.

The command to write the vision was based upon an anticipated delay in its fulfillment (see v. 3). In like manner, Isaiah had been told to write the name of his son upon a large tablet so that it might be preserved as a prophecy of the future downfall of Damascus and Samaria (Isa. 8:1-4). The writing down of a prophecy was a safeguard against its being forgotten or misunderstood. Even more important, it was a witness to its authenticity.

Habakkuk was told to write the vision plainly, "so he may run who reads it." An alternate translation of this final clause is, "so that even he that runs may read it." Those who prefer this second translation interpret the passage to mean that the tablets were to be erected in public places, such as the streets of Jerusalem, its public squares, or its Temple courts. This would enable those who hurried by—perhaps on a journey or on their way to work or to worship—to read at a glance and to retain the message.

I prefer the first translation, "so he may run who reads it." It was common in ancient Palestine for important messages to be sent by runners. These were chosen for their fleetness of foot and for their stamina (see 1 Sam. 4:10-18; 2 Sam. 18:19-33; Isa. 52:7-10). According to this interpretation, the vision about to be given to Habakkuk was so important that it needed to be heralded abroad. Therefore, the prophet was to entrust it to runners who would proclaim it throughout the land.

Verse 3 reinforces the idea that the prophet was warned in advance that the vision soon to be given to him might be delayed in its fulfillment. The delayed fulfillment of divine promises was a problem with which many of the Old Testament saints wrestled. It began as early as Abraham (Gen. 15:1-6) and continued throughout Old Testament times. New Testament Christians wrestled with the same problem (see 2 Pet. 3:3-10). It is addressed, among other places, in Hebrews 11, with its succinct statement that the saints of old "all died in faith, not having received the promises" (Heb. 11:13a, KJV). The Lord, in announcing to Habakkuk the delay in the fulfillment of the vision, was seeking to prepare him to live faithfully without the fulfillment. That he learned this lesson is evident in 3:17-19.

We also need to learn that to live by faith means to be willing to live with only a promise. "Standing on the promises" should be more than just a slogan with us; it should express the very essence of our fellowship with God. Are we willing to launch out like Abraham or to wait patiently like Habakkuk when all we have to go on is a promise? Are we willing to risk all for God when our only security is his word? Unless we can answer in the affirmative, we have not even begun to learn what it means to walk by faith.

The effect of verses 1-3 is to heighten the reader's suspense regarding the contents of the vision. When at last it is given in verses 4-5, we are prepared for a message of extraordinary proportions, and we are not disappointed! The ancient rabbis showed their regard for this passage by observing that Moses gave the Israelites 613 commandments. But, they said, David reduced them to eleven (Ps. 15), Isaiah to six (Isa. 33:15-16), Micah to three (Mic. 6:8), Isaiah again to two (Isa. 56:1), and Habakkuk to one (v. 4).[2]

The argument of verses 4-5, briefly stated, is this: there is a marked difference between the character and, therefore, the destiny of the righteous and the wicked. The wicked in this context refers to the Chaldeans and the righteous to the faithful remnant in Judah. The Chaldeans were doomed to failure because their souls were not upright in them (v. 4a; see also Ps. 18:25-26). Corrupt in their souls, defiant toward God, cruel and vindictive toward other nations, and possessed of a greed as wide as Sheol (v. 5; see also Isa. 5:14; Prov. 27:20), they lacked the moral integrity which alone ensures stability. The faithful in Judah, on the other hand, in spite of the outward circumstances of their lives, possessed the fidelity and moral integrity which gave permanence to their existence. These verses, therefore, are a summons to the faithful to live in a world where evil abounds and not to be overcome by it. They are a call to the righteous to maintain undivided allegiance to God, even when there are no immediate rewards or satisfactions. To do so means that one is following the path that leads to life.

"The righteous by his faithfulness shall live" (v. 4, author). This is the order followed in the Hebrew text of 2:4b. Let us briefly examine each of these elements in order.

First of all, what does it mean to be righteous? Righteousness in the Old Testament context has a social orientation. The righteous person is not merely the religious person, the temperate person, or the moral person. Rather he is the person who shows compassion toward the poor, the widow, the orphan, and the stranger. He is the one who never takes advantage of another's misfortune but protests loudly whenever others do so. He is the one who does everything possible to build a just and lasting society. Habakkuk was saying, That is what it means to live! Seek that and you shall live; ignore that, and there will be chaos and ruin.

The word rendered "faith" in the phrase, "by his faith," comes from a verb whose basic meaning is "to be steady, faithful, dependable, sure." It is used in Exodus 17:12 to refer to Moses' upraised arms as "steady." Isaiah 33:6 calls the Lord "the stability of your times." Psalm 78:37 condemns the Israelites because "their heart was not steadfast" toward the Lord. Psalm 93:5 says that the decrees of the Lord are "very sure." In 2 Chronicles 20:20, those who trust in the Lord are told that they will be "established." These passages all make use of the same verb root with which we are dealing in Habakkuk 2:4b.

To render the noun in Habakkuk 2:4b as "faith," with its usual connotation of "believing," is an inadequate translation. The person envisioned here is not merely the one who *has faith*, but the one who *is faithful*. The noun, therefore, should properly be rendered as "faithfulness." The same word is often used to describe the faithfulness of God (see Deut. 32:43; Ps. 36:4; 40:10; 100:5; Lam. 3:23). Hosea applied it to faithfulness to the covenant relationship (Hos. 2:20).

Faithfulness, when applied to God, means that he is trustworthy, firm, dependable, and sure. When applied to believers, it means not only that they regard God as absolutely trustworthy but also that they commit themselves unreservedly to him. The word is inclusive of the concepts of trust and obedience. The "faith" of a person or of a people is validated by their "faithfulness." The faith/faithfulness that God expects of the righteous, therefore, is not to be taken lightly. It speaks in the imperative mood. It offers no haven for the undecided and the uncommitted. It calls for stouthearted men and women to withstand the onslaughts of a hostile world and never waver in their commitment to God. A faith like that will guide brave souls into the way of life.

What did Habakkuk mean when he wrote that the righteous through their faithfulness would live? In Hebrew thought, to live meant more than merely to exist. Life was synonymous with prosperity, health, wholeness, and vitality. For example, the verb "to live" could mean to be healed (see Josh. 5:8), to recover from an illness (see Isa. 38:21), or to be restored to life (see Ps. 30:3). To have life meant to be vital and active. Fresh, running water, for example, was called "living water," in contrast to stagnant cistern water (see Jer. 2:13; 17:13). Likewise, wild animals were called "living animals," to distinguish them from tame and relatively lifeless barnyard animals.

Death, on the other hand, represented a state of weakness and inactivity (see Isa. 14:10). It was the opposite of life and vitality. Death was what Habakkuk had in mind when he said that those whose souls were not upright in them would fail (2:4a). Verse 5 enlarges upon the Babylonians' insatiable lust for power and conquest. Inflamed by wine, they launched campaign after campaign against other nations. They willed death to their victims; but in the end, it was they and not their victims who tasted the meaning of failure and death.

In summary, God's answer to Habakkuk's complaint was that pride and oppression lead to destruction, whereas integrity and faithfulness lead to life everlasting. The answer did not change the prophet's outward circumstances but was designed to change his attitude toward those circumstances. The Babylonians continued to hold the reins of world power and to rule in a cruel and vindictive way. Judah still lay under their control and the worst was yet to come; Jerusalem would soon be wiped out and its people taken into captivity. In just such a situation, God declared that evil was self-destructive and that righteousness alone would ultimately prevail.

Taunts Against the Chaldeans
2:6-20

This section consists of a series of five taunts or woes uttered against an oppressor. They were spoken by those who had been victims of oppression (v. 6). They teach that tyranny is suicidal and that the oppressor destroys himself. Other series of woe speeches are found in Isaiah 5:8-23; 10:1-4; 28:1; 29:15; 30:1; 31:1; 33:1; and

Amos 5:18; 6:1,4. Habakkuk's five taunts are all condemnatory in nature and constitute a cry of anger and dismay, or, as verse 6 states it, of "scoffing derision."

Since there are no definite historical references in this section, it is not altogether clear to whom the woe accusations were addressed. Were they addressed to some unknown oppressor? Were they addressed to Jehoiakim, king of Judah? Or were they addressed to Nebuchadnezzar, king of Babylon?

The latter possibility is the one adopted here. It is my opinion that the five woes serve to justify the severity of God's judgment against the Babylonians. Although the woes are addressed to the king as an individual, this is only because his policies represented those of the nation. In a real sense, he was the personification of the nation.

The themes that appear in this section are depressingly familiar to all of us. They include greed which is never satisfied, power which is used solely for selfish purposes, taking advantage of the weak and defenseless members of society, self-indulgence, the callous corruption of one's neighbors, and the worship of the works of one's own hands. Such behavior was suicidal in Habakkuk's day—and still is! Those who commit such deeds carry within themselves the seeds of their own destruction.

Against Greed and Violence (2:6-8)

The first woe is related to the greed of the Babylonians and their eagerness to enrich themselves at the expense of others. They conquered nation after nation, exacting from them huge contributions of money, men, and materials, thus heaping up what was not theirs.

"How long!" the victims of Babylonian oppression cried out (v. 6). This was the same bitter cry of lament that burst forth from Habakkuk's lips at the beginning of his book (1:2).

The reference to "pledges" (v. 6b) means that Babylon was being likened to a moneylender who exacted exorbitant pledges from his debtors. Verse 7 predicts a debtors' revolt. The exploited peoples would rise up, and Babylon would become booty for them. She who had spoiled others would herself be spoiled, and her violence would be brought to an end.

Against a False Sense of Security (2:9-11)

In the second woe saying, the king of Babylon is represented under the figure of an unscrupulous man who builds his house with "evil gain" (v. 9). This means that he financed his building projects by robbing and murdering and "cutting off many peoples" (v. 10).

All of this activity was aimed at providing a place that was secure, a place that was "safe from the reach of harm" (v. 9). As an eagle builds its nest on high to avoid attack (v. 9; see also Num. 24:21; Obad. 4), so the Babylonians sought to make themselves invulnerable to all threats. It is the curse of oppressor nations that they never feel secure but must always work feverishly to strengthen their defenses.

The Babylonians would soon learn, however, that security built upon the exploitation of other nations is an illusion. The prophet stated it very simply: "you have forfeited your life" (v. 10). The literal meaning of the Hebrew is "you have missed the mark." Instead of bringing them honor and satisfaction, their deeds would only bring them shame and humiliation. The abiding truth of this passage is that there is no honor or security for a nation built upon the exploitation and oppression of other nations. That nation, like Babylon, may set its nest on high, but in the end it will come crashing to the earth.

According to verse 11, a house built upon oppression is a haunted house. From its stone walls come cries of distress, answered by similar cries from the woodwork. One is reminded of the blood of Abel crying out for vengeance from the ground where it had been spilled (Gen. 4:10) or of the wages of the poor crying out against dishonest landlords (Jas. 5:4). The oppressor is never able to escape his deeds, least of all when he is alone in his own house.

Against Disregard for Human Lives (2:12-14)

The third woe continues the use of building metaphors to describe the horrible deeds committed by the Babylonians. They are represented as building a city using iniquity for a foundation and blood for building blocks. A similar accusation was lodged against Jehoiakim by the prophet Jeremiah (Jer. 22:13-17). Habakkuk was probably referring to the grandiose plans of Nebuchadnezzar to build Babylon. This involved the forced labor of countless thousands of war captives, both Jews and Gentiles, who were driven by heartless taskmasters. The building costs were paid by stripping conquered lands of their wealth.

Babylon did not count on having to answer to the God of Israel. He has decreed that civilizations built upon violence and oppression will perish by fire and that nations that live by exploiting others will have nothing to show for their labors (v. 13). God has always intervened in history to prevent the permanent success of nations that oppose him (see Gen. 11:1-9).

Verse 14 gives an additional reason for the overthrow of oppressors. It is that their cruel and selfish domination of the world is a denial of God's purpose in creation. That purpose is that the knowledge of his glory should cover the earth as the waters cover the sea. There is simply not room enough on earth for a kingdom like that of Babylon, built upon violence and oppression, and God's kingdom of peace and righteousness.

Against the Corruption of One's Neighbors (2:15-17)

The fourth woe again takes up the theme of drunkenness (see 2:5). The king of Babylon is compared to a man who gives poisonous or intoxicating drinks to his neighbors. He does this not as a friendly gesture but in order to exploit them and to gaze on their shame, or nakedness (see Gen. 9:20-22).

The punishment of the Babylonians was that they would be forced to drink from the cup of the Lord's wrath until they were overcome by it and shame covered their glory (v. 16). The atrocities they had done to others would return to plague them (v. 17). "The violence done to Lebanon" probably refers to the stripping of the forests of Lebanon during Nebuchadnezzar's rebuilding of Babylon. What had been done to the forests and to the wild beasts, as well as to cities and those who dwelled in them, was but a foreshadowing of what would happen to Babylon itself (v. 17).

Against the Worship of Idols (2:18-20)

The fifth and final woe is a stern condemnation of idolatry. In this instance, the word "woe" is not found at the beginning but in the middle of the oracle (v. 19). This passage, written a half century later, may be compared to the classic attack on idolatry in Isaiah 44:9-10. Both passages were inspired by the idolatrous worship of the Babylonians.

Verse 18 opens with a rhetorical question, that is, a question with an implied or predetermined answer. That answer is that an idol is of no profit whatsoever to those who worship it or seek instruction from it. It will always prove to be "a teacher of lies" (v. 18). Praying to an idol is also an exercise in futility. It is nothing more than trying to arouse a piece of wood or a block of stone (v. 19; see also 1 Kings 18:25-29). While it may be overlaid with gold and silver, it has no life-giving breath within it.

In contrast to these dumb and lifeless idols, God is alive and real and rules over all the nations from his throne on high. It behooves all the earth, therefore, to keep silence before him (v. 20). It is significant that Habakkuk ended his series of taunts against Babylon with a universal call to worship.

I have occasionally attended churches where the words of verse 20 were written over the entrance to the sanctuary. It is almost a misuse of this verse to use it in this manner. Far from meaning that the Lord is present in a temple somewhere on earth and that those who enter this temple must show proper reverence for him, the verse emphatically denies that any temple on earth is capable of holding him. They may hold idols of metal, wood, or stone (vv. 18-19) but not the living Lord. The temple from which he rules over the earth is certainly not the Temple in Jerusalem. Rather, it is his "holy temple," that is, his heavenly temple (v. 20). The command to keep silence is addressed, therefore, not to a small band of faithful followers gathered in some earthly sanctuary. It is not even addressed primarily to the Lord's people. It is addressed instead to "all the earth" and in the present context refers especially to the idolatrous oppressors of the Israelites, the Babylonians. It is they who should have realized the futility of idolatry and bowed in silence before the omnipotent and omnipresent Lord. The only adequate place for this call to worship to be displayed would be across the face of the heavens where all nations might see it and bow in reverence.

The Prayer of Habakkuk
3:1-19

Title (3:1)

The title, together with other musical notations in the middle and at the end of this chapter, suggests that it may have been composed to be performed by the Temple choirs. It is called a prayer of Habakkuk, "according to Shigionoth." The last word is found only here and in its singular form in the title to Psalm 7: "A Shiggaion of David." Its exact meaning is uncertain. Some have related it to the verb "to reel," interpreting it as a song to be sung with great excitement and rhythmic motions.

Three times within the body of the prayer the word *selah* occurs (vv. 3,9,13). It also is a musical notation and should never be translated. It occurs seventy-one times in the Psalms, being present in thirty-one different psalms. The most widely held theory as to its meaning is that it marked the place where the musicians either increased the tempo of the music or played a musical interlude while the singers paused.

The notation at the end assigns the prayer "to the choirmaster." This notation appears in the titles of fifty-five of the psalms. It is also stated at the end that Habakkuk's prayer is to be performed "with stringed instruments." This phrase is found also in five of the titles to psalms. It is entirely possible that at one time this prayer may have belonged to a larger collection of Temple songs.

The Prophet's Petition (3:2)

The actual prayer or petition in chapter 3 is very brief. It begins with the prophet's simple statement: "O Lord, I have heard the report of thee,/and thy work, O Lord, do I fear."

It is interesting to note that the same verb, "I have heard," occurs in verse 2 and again in verse 16, where it is translated "I hear." It, therefore, forms the framework around the mighty appearance of God in judgment and redemption described in verses 3-15. Its first occurrence refers to God's mighty deeds in the past, doubtlessly an allusion to the Exodus experience of Israel, deeds which the prophet knew only from hearsay and would like to see repeated in his day. Coming immediately after this petition is a vision of God's intervention to save his people and to crush his foes (vv. 3-15).

After the vision, the prophet spoke again and confessed, "I hear— I will quietly wait" (v. 16). His prayer for a fresh manifestation of God's power had been answered, and he was satisfied. Thus the book comes to a climax in the prophet's personal resignation to the divine will. He was willing at last to commit to God the judgment of the Babylonians and to trust him to bring it about in his own good time (v. 16b). What the prophet's commitment meant in day-to-day living is described in verses 17-19.

Habakkuk's petition shows that he believed he was living in an in-between time, so far as the mighty acts of God were concerned. He had heard of God's mighty acts, and these were still celebrated in the Passover (Deut. 16:1-12) and confessed by worshiping Israelites (Deut. 26:5-10). But the events surrounding the Exodus and the conquest lay five full centuries in the past. What of the present? The thing that troubled Habakkuk most was God's apparent inactivity in the present. It was of little comfort to him to be told that God would repeat his wonders in the distant future. He had to live his life in the now, in that painful interval between the remembered past and the expected future. And so he prayed for God to renew his work "in the midst of the years" (v. 2).

Habakkuk's words are also relevant to the in-between times that we experience, both as the people of God and as individual Christians. We also live in that middle period between Christ's incarnation and his second coming. If we are to meet God in any meaningful way, it must be in the here and now. Just as it afforded little comfort to the prophet to be told that he lived between a glorious past and a bright future, even so we long to see a renewal of God's mighty acts in our world and during our lifetime. Habakkuk's example should encourage us also to pray for a renewal of God's marvelous deeds "in the midst of the years."

The final petition in verse 2, "in wrath remember mercy," suggests that Habakkuk regarded the moment in history in which he lived as under the wrath of God, whereas the past, and particularly the time of the Exodus, was under God's grace. Therefore he petitioned God to remember past mercies in this moment of wrath. To remember means to actualize, to bring up-to-date, to repeat. Thus he reinforced his earlier petition that God would renew his mighty deeds in his day.

God's Self-Revelation (3:3-15)

In answer to Habakkuk's prayer, there came to him a vision of God's intervention on behalf of his people. The vision contains many allusions to the Exodus, particularly to the deliverance at the Red Sea and to the wilderness wanderings. References to God's victory over rivers (vv. 8a,9b), the sea (vv. 8b,15a), the raging waters (v. 10b), the deep (v. 10c), and the surging of mighty waters (v. 15b) would all serve as reminders of his earlier victory over Pharaoh's forces at the Red Sea (see Ex. 15:1; Pss. 77:6-14; 114:3,5). The period of wilderness wanderings is reflected in the references to Teman and Mount Paran (v. 3a), both located west of Edom near the Gulf of Akaba. The mention of Cushan and Midian (v. 7) is also significant, for they were desert tribes hostile to the wandering Israelites (see Num. 25:17; Judg. 6—7). By the use of such imagery borrowed from the past, the prophet was saying that God was about to intervene in history and repeat his mighty acts of deliverance on behalf of his people. And this was precisely what the prophet had prayed for (v. 2).

Some have interpreted the vision of verses 3-15 as but a recounting of past events, a recollection of God's mighty deeds in the long ago. But the majority of the verbs found here are perfects, and I interpret them as future perfects or perfects of certainty. The prophet was so sure that God would act to put down his foes and save his people that he described it as if it had already happened. This is the only interpretation that makes sense of the prophet's response to the vision as recorded in verse 16b: "I will quietly wait for the day of trouble/to come upon people who invade us."

An appearance of God, such as we find in this passage, is known as a theophany, which simply means an appearance or manifestation of God. Theophanies are common in the Old Testament and are often reported in hymnic forms that make wide use of poetic imagery and symbolism (see Deut. 33:2-5; Judg. 5:4-5; Pss. 18:7-15; 68:7-10; 77:16-20; 97:1-5; 114:1-8; Isa. 6:1-5; Ezek. 1:4-28). In most theophanies, the Lord comes from afar. His coming is accompanied by mighty upheavals in nature, such as fire, wind, flood, earthquake, and the darkening of the sun and moon. The reason for the Lord's appearing is to tread down his foes and to save his people. The theophanic hymns were written to be sung by the people in celebration of their deliverance by the mighty hand of God.

Habakkuk spoke of God as coming from Teman, a desert region south of Judah and northwest of Edom (v. 3). His coming was signaled by a dazzling light (v. 4). Pestilence and plague went out from him (v. 5). The earth reeled and quaked (v. 6). The tribes of the desert were in dismay (v. 7). Rivers broke forth in new places on the earth (v. 9). The high mountains and the great deep were in distress (v. 10). The sun and the moon ceased to shine when God's great light appeared (v. 11). God trampled the nations in his fury (v. 12), rescuing his people from the strong hand of the enemy (v. 13). He smashed the heads of the warriors who were threatening his people with destruction (v. 14). He rode to victory against the sea and the mighty surging waters (v. 15). Such was Habakkuk's vision of the coming of the Lord to put down the Babylonians and to exalt his people.

There is a marked parallel between Job and Habakkuk. Both wrestled with deep doubts related to God's seeming inactivity and his absence from the world when his people needed him most. In neither instance did God provide logical or rational answers to the expressed doubts. But he did appear to Job and to Habakkuk and his self-revelation gave to each a new perspective to live by. There burst from Job's lips this confession, "I had heard of thee by the hearing of the ear,/but now my eye sees thee;/therefore I despise myself and/repent in dust and ashes" (Job 42:5-6). Habakkuk's response was equally as dramatic and will be the subject of the final section of the commentary.

The Prophet's Response (3:16-19)

Habakkuk's response to the vision of the Lord's appearing to judge the Babylonians and to save his people came in several stages. First, there was an overpowering fear and a feeling of helplessness. He cried out, "I hear, and my body trembles,/my lips quiver at the sound; rottenness enters into my bones,/my steps totter beneath me" (v. 16a). Habakkuk's reaction was not unlike that of others who had similar visions of God in all his glory and majesty. Moses hid his face as he stood before the burning bush, "for he was afraid to look at God" (Ex. 3:6). When Isaiah saw God seated upon his throne, he cried out, "Woe is me! For I am lost" (Isa. 6:5). Ezekiel caught a vision of God riding across the heavens in his celestial chariot, and he fell upon his face in wonder and awe (Ezek. 1:24). It is not surprising that Habakkuk's body trembled, his lips quivered, and his legs could no longer support him. It was an awesome experience to stand in the presence of the Almighty.

The second stage in Habakkuk's response was his submission to the will of God with respect to the final judgment of the Babylonians. Earlier God had enjoined him that if the vision of retribution for evildoers and reward for the righteous should be delayed in its fulfillment, he should wait for it (2:3). Almost at the end of his book the prophet responded, "I will quietly wait for the day of trouble/to come upon people who invade us" (v. 16b). He recognized that the Babylonians had a lot of rope, but he believed that the end of the rope was held securely in the hands of God. And believing that, he could trust God to judge them in his own good time.

The third and climactic stage in the prophet's response to God's self-revelation was his unconditional trust in God, reflected in one of the greatest confessions of faith that has ever been made (vv. 17-19). He had earlier complained to God about the hardships he and his people were suffering at the hands of their foes. But now he was able to say that if there should be complete crop failure in the land, leaving him without food and forcing him to face starvation, even so he would still rejoice in the Lord.

It was not that the prophet doubted for a moment that God was able to give all these things in abundance. He, like Jeremiah, had surely been nurtured on the Book of Deuteronomy, with its clear statement that it was God who blessed his people with the produce of the fields (Deut. 8:7-10; 28:2-14). Habakkuk did not doubt that God *could* give these things. Rather, his faith was such that it enabled him to say in effect, "Though he withhold that which he is able to give, yet will I trust him." He was grateful for all favors but dependent upon none. So long as he knew the Giver, he could be unconcerned about the gifts. God had become the supreme reality of his life and fellowship with him was all that ultimately mattered. He had finally learned what it meant for the just to live by faith.

The final verse of the prophecy sounds the note of strength and security. The prophet could overcome insurmountable obstacles and climb inaccessible heights because the Lord was his strength. These words can best be understood by comparing them with David's song of trust in 2 Samuel 22 (repeated in Ps. 18): "God is my strong refuge/and has made my way safe./He made my feet like hinds' feet,/and set me secure on the heights./Thou didst give a wide place for my steps under me,/and my feet did not slip" (v. 33-34,37).

Notes

1. Donald E. Gowan, *The Triumph of Faith in Habakkuk* (Atlanta: John Knox Press, 1976), p. 38.

2. Ibid., p. 11.

ZEPHANIAH

Introduction

The Prophet

Nothing is known about Zephaniah except what we learn from his book. Here he emerges as a superb poet and a stern preacher of righteousness. His vivid portrayal of the Day of the Lord as a day of harsh wrath reminds us of the preaching of Jonathan Edwards in the early days of our own country. Zephaniah is depicted in medieval art as the prophet with the lantern of the Lord, searching out sinners for destruction (see 1:12). He reminds us more of Amos than of Hosea.

According to the title in 1:1, Zephaniah was active during the reign of Josiah, which would place his ministry somewhere between 640 and 609 BC. The title also traces his ancestry back through four generations to a great-great-grandfather named Hezekiah. Since most prophetic books list only the prophet's father (see Isa. 1:1; Jer. 1:1; Ezek. 1:3; Hos. 1:1), there must have been a special reason for tracing Zephaniah's lineage back to Hezekiah. I agree with those who interpret this as meaning that this was the same Hezekiah who ruled over Judah from 715 to 687 BC. That would mean Zephaniah was of royal blood and was related to King Josiah as second cousin. It is perhaps significant that while he condemned the corrupt officials of the court he never included the king in his condemnations.

It is generally agreed that Jerusalem was the home of the prophet and his sphere of activity. This is shown by the fact that he was aware of the religious and moral conditions of the city (see 1:4-6,8-9,12; 3:1-7) and was familiar with its landmarks (see 1:10-11). Like Isaiah before him, he was God's politician, sent to turn the capital of Judah from the path of destruction.

Zephaniah means "the Lord hides" or "the Lord protects." Assuming that he was born during the reign of Manasseh, he may have been given this name as a sign of his parents' faith in the power of the Lord to protect. He was the first canonical prophet to follow

Isaiah and his preaching signaled the rebirth of prophecy after more than seventy years of silence.

Date and Background

The Assyrians devastated the land of Judah in 701 BC, capturing forty-six of her fortified cities. After that, Judah was firmly under the control of Assyria. Assyrian influence was especially strong during the reigns of Manasseh (687-642 BC) and Amon (642-640 BC). The religious life of the people suffered greatly from foreign influence (see 2 Kings 21:1-26).

After Amon was murdered in 640 BC, Josiah was placed on the throne, although he was only eight years of age (2 Kings 22:1). Many of the officials who sponsored him during his minor years were still heavily influenced by Assyrian culture and religion. Zephaniah accused them of wearing foreign clothes and of ignoring the demands of justice in their public administration (1:8-9). He also accused the people of trying to worship pagan deities and the Lord God of Israel at the same time (1:4-6). Zephaniah's task was made all the more urgent by the moral and spiritual corruption that Manasseh had brought to the land.

The generally accepted view is that Zephaniah prophesied during the early part of Josiah's reign, before the king had initiated his political and religious reforms. Already in this early period the Assyrian Empire was threatening to break up. Zephaniah could confidently predict the downfall of Nineveh (2:13-15), a prophecy that was fulfilled in 612 BC. A more precise date for the prophet would be somewhere between 630-625 BC, about the same time that Jeremiah began his ministry.

The Message of the Book

The message of Zephaniah is characterized by its sternness. It emphasizes the justice of the Lord more than his mercy. The book announces the destruction of sinners but offers no prayer of intercession on their behalf. The frequent references to fire in its brief pages led George Adam Smith, to write: "No hotter book lies in the Old Testament. Neither dew nor grass nor tree nor any blossom lives in it, but everywhere is fire, smoke, and darkness, drifting chaff, ruins, nettles, saltpits, with owls and ravens looking down from the windows of desolate palaces."[1]

The central concept in the message of Zephaniah is the Day of the

Lord. The watchword of the book is that the Day of the Lord is "near and hastening fast" (1:14; see also v. 7). It is called "the day of the Lord's sacrifice" (1:8) and "a day of wrath" (1:15,18; 2:2-3). Other terms used to describe it are "distress and anguish," "ruin and devastation," "darkness and gloom," "clouds and thick darkness," and "trumpet blast and battle cry" (1:15-16). The prophet understood that day as a kind of spiritual D day, a spectacular day of judgment on which sinners were to be destroyed and a purified remnant spared.

It is interesting to note the kinds of sins which Zephaniah condemned. In contrast to the eighth-century prophets, he said very little about social sins. Rather, he condemned the sins of false worship (1:4-6), of vanity (1:8), of complacency (1:12), of pride (2:1,10; 3:11), of rebellion (3:1), of self-sufficiency (2:15; 3:2), of greed (3:3-4), and of obstinate unbelief (3:7).

The quality that Zephaniah valued most in men and women was humility. Only the humble would be spared on the day of the Lord's wrath (2:3). After the judgment had passed, the proud would be no more, but there would be left in Jerusalem a people humble and lowly, one that sought refuge in the name of the Lord (3:12). From these humble folk, God would rebuild his kingdom. This is the nearest the Old Testament comes to saying, "Blessed are the poor in spirit, for theirs is the kingdom of heaven. Blessed are the meek, for they shall inherit the earth" (Matt. 5:3,5).

It should be noted that the only hope Zephaniah envisioned lay beyond the day of judgment. In the last chapter, the message turns from threats to promises and looks forward to a day of healing and liberation after the day of wrath. Zephaniah's task was to lead his people to repentance, obedience, and humility, so that God might restore them to his favor.

The Day of the Lord Against Judah
1:1 to 2:4

Title (1:1)

Zephaniah means "the Lord hides" or "the Lord protects." This verse places his ministry in the days of Josiah (640-609 BC). He

probably preached somewhere between 630 and 625 BC, while
Josiah was quite young and before he had begun his reforms.

It is unusual for a prophet's lineage to be traced back four
generations. This has led to speculation that Zephaniah's great-great-
grandfather, here called Hezekiah, was the king who ruled
Jerusalem in the days of Isaiah. This seems to be a valid assumption,
although it cannot be proven from the text.

Judgment on a Cosmic Scale (1:2-3)

The opening statement of the book forecasts judgment on a
worldwide scale. It is a harsh word of judgment untempered by any
suggestion of hope or any summons to repentance. It must have had
a tremendous shock value.

What Zephaniah preached was a return of the world to chaos, an
undoing of God's work of creation (see also Jer. 4:23-26). The
background to these verses is to be found in Genesis 6—9, the story
of Noah and the Flood. After the Flood, God promised that he
would never again curse the ground and never again destroy all
living creatures (Gen. 8:21). Zephaniah used the very same Hebrew
word to say that God would indeed destroy ("utterly sweep away")
everything from the face of the earth (vv. 2-3). It sounds almost as if
God had reversed his position and had decided to bring a new flood
of judgment over the earth.

Special Classes to Be Judged (1:4-13)

Judah and Jerusalem would be the first to feel the Lord's hand in
judgment. Certain groups within the chosen nation were singled out
for special condemnation.

Priests Who Promote False Worship (1:4-6)

This is not the usual word for priests but one which refers to
idolatrous priests who parade as true priests of the Lord (see 2 Kings
23:5; Hos. 10:5). They had polluted the worship of the Lord by
combining it with the worship of Baal (v. 4), of the hosts of heaven

(v. 5*a*), and of Milcom (v. 5*b*). The people of Judah were apparently trying to play it safe by staying on the good side of all the gods. They failed to realize that their God demanded undivided loyalty.

Officials Who Copy Foreign Customs and Practice Oppression (1:7-9)

This section opens with the strong interjection, "Be silent!" This abrupt command often accompanies a revelation of the majesty and power of the Lord, especially as he comes to judge (see Neh. 8:11; Amos 6:10; Hab. 2:20; Zech. 2:13).

The coming Day of the Lord is compared to a sacrifice, a figure of speech not uncommon in the prophets (see Isa. 34:6; Jer. 46:10; Ezek. 39:17). The word for sacrifice means a blood sacrifice, that is, an animal sacrifice, as opposed to a vegetable sacrifice. In this case, the sacrificial victim is Israel and the invited guests are the enemies of Israel.

Among those marked for slaughter on the day of the Lord's sacrifice are the court officials, who deck themselves in foreign attire, "every one who leaps over the threshold," and who practice "violence and fraud" (vv. 8-9). The second of these accusations is much debated as to its meaning. It may refer to forcible entry into the home of the poor in order to rob and to plunder. Or it may refer to some superstitious practice connected with entering a sanctuary, such as leaping over the threshold in order to avoid contact with the resident deity (see 1 Sam. 5:1-5). Others interpret it as referring to some form of idol worship. The officials may have been worshiping false gods.

Merchants Who Accumulate Great Wealth (1:10-11)

These verses refer to a number of places within Jerusalem which cannot be precisely identified. The Fish Gate is thought to have been in the north wall of the city, facing Tyre (see Neh. 3:3; 12:39; 2 Chron. 33:14). The Second Quarter may have been a new addition to the old Jebusite city (see 2 Kings 22:14). The Mortar may have been a marketplace where the merchants displayed their wares.

The word used for merchant is "Canaanite" since the Canaanites (also called Phoenicians) were the chief merchants of the ancient Near East. Even Israelite merchants came to be known as "Canaanites," which probably meant no more than "traders."

Zephaniah predicted that the merchants would bear the brunt of the coming judgment and would be stripped of their treasures of silver. He probably was thinking about an invasion by a foe from the north, hence the references to the north side of the city.

Skeptics Who Grow Smug and Complacent (1:12-13)

The Lord announced that he would light lamps and search out for punishment those who thought they could live as they pleased and he would do nothing about it. They did not consider him to be active and effective but regarded him as a do-nothing God. They were practical atheists in that they lived as if God did not exist.

The phrase used to describe their complacency is "thickening upon their lees" (v. 12). When wine was allowed to stand too long before being poured off from the sediment of the wine vat, it became over sweet and syrupy. "To settle upon one's lees" became a proverb for smugness, complacency, and muddled thinking (see Jer. 48:11).

Judgment would come upon these indifferent and skeptical persons in the form of an invasion. Their houses would be destroyed and their goods plundered. The latter half of verse 13 describes their judgment by means of a futility curse. They would labor but without being able to enjoy the fruits of their labor. Sometimes the wages of sin is utter futility. The sinner works hard but has nothing to show for it (see Amos 5:11).

A Day of Wrath Against the Whole Earth
(1:14-18)

Its Rapid Approach (1:14)

Zephaniah broadened the concept of the Day of the Lord to make it apply to all nations. His words were designed to awaken terror in his listeners. The rapidly approaching Day of the Lord would mean the end of human history and the destruction of the earth.

Its Terrifying Effects (1:15-16)

Words are piled on each other in these verses to describe the terror of the Day of the Lord. The famous Latin hymn, *Dies Irae, Dies Illa* borrows its title from the opening words of verse 15, "A day of wrath is that day."

In language reminiscent of Amos 5:18-20, Zephaniah pictured that day as a day of distress and anguish, of ruin and devastation, of darkness and gloom, of clouds and thick darkness, of trumpet blast and battle cry. The indications are strong that he had in mind the terror and devastation caused by an invading army.

Its Inescapable Destruction (1:17-18)

The fury of that day will be focused on those who have sinned against the Lord. Their destruction will be both horrible and inescapable. It will be so horrible that their blood will be poured out as if it had no more value than dust and their flesh as if it were as cheap as dung. It will be so inescapable that neither silver nor gold will avail to deliver sinners from the wrath of the Lord. All the earth will be consumed and all the inhabitants of the earth will come to an end.

An Urgent Call to Repentance (2:1-4)

Warning to the Shameless (2:1-2)

The threat against Judah (1:2-18) is followed by a call for her to repent. It is an urgent call since the decree of the Lord was about to be implemented. She was addressed as a shameless nation, or as rendered by *The New English Bible*, an "unruly nation" (v. 1). Israel was usually addressed as a "people"; for her to be addressed as a "nation" was a deliberate insult. This is the word normally applied to pagan peoples.

Encouragement to the Humble (2:3)

This verse calls upon the faithful remnant, here described as all the "humble of the land," to seek the Lord. Repeating the same verb, it also exhorted them to seek righteousness and humility. The dominant view of the Book of Zephaniah is that the poor and humble people are the truly righteous, whereas the proud and haughty are the enemies of the Lord (see 3:11-13).

The possibility held up before the humble who truly seek the Lord is that they might perhaps "be hidden on the day of the wrath of the Lord." The word "perhaps" is important; for even the righteous humble have no binding claim on God's protection. The ultimate decision about who may be spared rests solely with him.

A Lesson from the Philistines (2:4)

The call to Judah to repent is reinforced by a forecast of the doom of the Philistines. Their cities are to be destroyed, and their destruction should serve as a warning to Judah.

Prophecies Against the Nations
2:5-15

The second major section of Zephaniah deals with the impact of the day of the Lord on the nations. The sequence of these oracles of judgment follows the point of the compass. First to be condemned were Israel's neighbors to the west, the Philistines (vv. 5-7). They were followed by those to the east, Moab and Ammon (vv. 8-11). Next came those to the south, the Ethiopians (v. 12). The list closes with those to the north, the Assyrians (vv. 13-15).

Against Philistia (2:5-7)

The Philistines had been enemies of the Israelites since both first set foot in the land of Canaan. During the period of the judges and in the early years of the monarchy, there was a seesaw struggle between these two peoples as to who would gain control over the land. Although the Israelites were largely victorious, they were never able in the pre-Exilic period to drive the Philistines completely out of the land. They continued to occupy the coastal plain just north of the border with Egypt.

The oracle against Philistia contains a promise that the remnant of the house of Judah would take possession of the lands and houses of the Philistines (v. 7). This promise anticipated the fuller description of Judah's restoration in the latter part of the book (3:9-20).

Against Moab and Ammon (2:8-11)

Moab and Ammon lay east of Judah beyond the Jordan. The two were separated by the river Arnon. According to Genesis 19:30-38, both were descendants of Lot through a "family planning program" initiated by his two daughters. Despite this tradition of kinship with the Israelites, the relationship between Israel and Moab, or Israel and Ammon, was seldom peaceful. Amos had earlier pronounced judgment against these two nations (Amos 1:13-15; 2:1-3).

The oracle against Moab and Ammon condemns them for their pride, their arrogance, and their disdain for the people of God (vv. 8-10). As punishment for their behavior, they would become like the proverbial cities of Sodom and Gomorrah, "possessed by nettles and salt pits,/and a waste for ever" (v. 9). Once again the promise was made that the remnant of the Lord's people would move in and take possession of these two lands (v. 9). This oracle closes with a prediction of the final eclipse of all the gods of the heathen. When this has occurred, every nation would bow down in recognition of the God of Israel (v. 11; see also Isa. 45:23; Rom. 14:11; Phil. 2:10).

Against Ethiopia (2:12)

The southern point of the compass is represented by Ethiopia, for which the Hebrew word is *Cush*. This oracle may in fact be directed against Egypt since it was ruled by a Cushite or Ethiopian dynasty from 715 to 663 BC. The pharaohs of this dynasty frequently interfered in the political and religious affairs of Judah (see Isa. 18—20; Jer. 46; Ezek. 29—32). One of these rulers, Pharaoh Neco II, slew King Josiah of Judah at Megiddo in 609 BC (see 2 Kings 23:29).

Against Assyria (2:13-15)

Zephaniah alloted more space to Assyria and its capital, Nineveh, than to any other foreign nation. This shows how important Assyria was still considered to be and gives further support to the suggestion that Zephaniah was active during the early years of Josiah. There is a close parallel between the language of this oracle and that of the Book of Nahum, which is also directed against Nineveh.

From being the proud capital of a vast empire, Nineveh would be reduced to a haunt of wild beasts and birds of prey (vv. 13-14). The identification of the animals and birds mentioned here is difficult, and the different translations offer a variety of suggestions. It is clear, however, that the prophet was referring to the types of animals and birds that inhabited the deserted ruins of ancient cities.

Nineveh was condemned for her pride and arrogant self-sufficiency (v. 15a). Pride of power and position is a besetting sin of strong nations and was resoundingly condemned by the prophets (see Isa. 14:12-20; 47:8-11; Jer. 48:28-30; 49:14-16; 50:29-32). In the end, Nineveh would become a desolation and all who passed by her would hiss and shake their fists (v. 15*b*; see also Nah. 3:19).

The Lord's Indignation Against Jerusalem
3:1-8

The prophet included Jerusalem among the nations who were to be judged, just as Amos had earlier included Judah and Israel at the end of his list (see Amos 2:4,6). Although Jerusalem is not mentioned by name, it is perfectly clear that the prophet had her in mind.

A Cruel and Headstrong City (3:1-2)

The word *woe* is used often in the Old Testament to introduce a lament. Zephaniah lamented because there was rebellion, defilement, and oppression in Jerusalem.

Four charges were made against the city in verse 2. (1) She had not listened to the word of God as spoken through her prophets (see Jer. 7:25-26; Amos 2:11-12). (2) She had refused to accept discipline or correction (see Jer. 2:30; 5:3; 7:28; 32:33). (3) She had not trusted God. (4) She had not drawn near to him in penitent worship.

Wicked Leaders and a Righteous God (3:3-5)

The leaders of the nation were condemned in this section. Jerusalem's officials were compared to roaring lions and her judges to evening wolves. The implied meaning is that they preyed on their own people (see Jer. 5:26-28; Ezek. 34:2-6; Mic. 3:1-3).

The religious leaders were no better than the political leaders (see Jer. 6:13-15). The priests profaned what was sacred, neglected to teach the Law, and did violence to it.

The Lord remained faithful even in the face of Jerusalem's failure and defilement. God was the one constant factor in the situation. He is righteous. He does no wrong. His justice shines forth as regularly as the dawning of each new day. Without the changelessness of God, there would be no future for the rebellious city.

An Unlearned Lesson (3:6-7)

These verses are a lament from the Lord over the failure of historical judgments to teach Judah repentance. God pointed to the destruction that had been wrought on other nations, apparently through the instrumentality of the Assyrians. Nations had been cut off and cities laid waste, and yet Jerusalem only pursued wickedness with renewed vigor. She had learned nothing from the judgments of history and all her history was the story of wasted opportunities.

Verse 7 sets forth the qualities God had hoped to see demonstrated in the life of the city. Here is provided an answer to the question, Who is a true worshiper of the Lord? First, a true worshiper fears the Lord (see also Job 28:28; Prov. 9:10). Second, he or she accepts correction (see v. 2). Third, he or she takes to heart the instruction of the Lord and profits from it. These were the qualities the Lord looked for in Jerusalem, but they were all sadly lacking.

Gathered to Be Judged (3:8)

The Lord counseled those who made up the faithful remnant and who were perplexed by the continuing evil in the world to have patience. Soon they would see the nations gathered together, meaning perhaps at Jerusalem, and the fire of the Lord devouring sinners. In this verse, the prophet returned to his favorite theme, which was the great and terrible Day of the Lord. The implication of

this verse is that sinners in Jerusalem were to perish along with all
the godless nations gathered from the ends of the earth.

Hope Beyond Judgment
3:9-20

One Language and One Worship (3:9-10)

God does not want judgment to be his final word. Even his
judgment is meant to be redemptive, and he wounds in order that
he might heal.

After God had gathered the nations to be judged, he would
redeem a portion of them, purifying their speech in order that they
might call on his name and serve him with one accord. Pure
offerings would be brought to him even from beyond the rivers of
Ethiopia, which in Zephaniah's day meant from the fartherest ends
of the earth.

Restoring pure speech to the nations brings to mind the confusion
of the speech of those who attempted to build the tower of Babel
(Gen. 11:1-9). Furthermore, whereas they were united in their
efforts to build a city and a tower and to make a name for
themselves, those whom the Lord purifies will be united in his
worship and will serve him "with one accord" (literally, "with one
shoulder"). The picture used here is that of several oxen yoked
together pulling a single plow.

The reference to offerings being brought to the Lord from beyond
the rivers of Ethiopia (v. 10) is in keeping with other prophecies,
such as Isaiah 19:18-25, Zechariah 14:16-19, and Malachi 1:11.

A New People for a New Age (3:11-13)

Zephaniah believed that the Day of the Lord was inevitable but
that after it had passed there would come a day of rejoicing for Israel

and Jerusalem. However, not all the Israelites would participate in
the restoration. Those who were proud and haughty would be
removed. The remnant would constitute the new people for a new
age.

The new people would possess those qualities which were
pleasing to the Lord. As summarized by the prophet, they included
an attitude of humility and lowliness, an eagerness to seek refuge in
the name of the Lord, a determination to do no wrong and to utter
no lies, and a commitment to be innocent and without deceit in
one's speech. A glorious future awaited those who possess these
qualifications. "For they shall pasture and lie down/and none shall
make them afraid" (v. 13b).

A Call to Rejoicing (3:11-18a)

The theme of this section is that Jerusalem was to sing and rejoice
because the Lord her King had cast down all her enemies and taken
up his dwelling place in her midst. He is a mighty warrior who gives
victory, and there would never be any further need for his people to
be in fear. This victory hymn is similar in structure and content to
many of the psalms that celebrate the Lord's kingship (see Ps. 47;
95—99; 149).

This section also bears certain likenesses to the "holy war"
passages found in the early pages of the Old Testament. Note
especially the references to the Lord casting out enemies (v. 15) and
assuming the role of a warrior to win victory for his people (v. 17).
Also to be included here are the exhortations to Israel not to fear nor
to let her hands grow weak (vv. 15-16). Finally, there is the call to join
in festive celebration (vv. 14,17-18a), a feature common also to the
holy war traditions (see Ex. 15:1-21; Judg. 5:1-31).

The Return of the Exiles (3:18b-20)

God spoke in these verses as the shepherd of his bruised and
battered flock. After the great and terrible Day of the Lord had
passed, he would gather his scattered sheep, take away their shame

and reproach, heal their wounds, put down their enemies, lead them home again, and completely restore their fortunes. This closing section presents a pleasant prospect. It is as if the noise of war had been hushed and the reign of true peace had begun. It is a condition that is best described by the Hebrew word *shalom*.

Note

1. George Adam Smith, *The Book of the Twelve Prophets,* Vol. II (New York and London: Harper and Brothers Publishers, 1928), p. 47.

HAGGAI

Introduction

The Prophet

Nothing is known about the personal life of Haggai except what we learn from his book and from brief references in Ezra 5:1 and 6:14. There is no way to determine how old he was when he began his ministry. His name is related to the Hebrew word *hag*, meaning "festival" or "holy day," which suggests that he may have been born on such a day. It is likely that he was born in Babylon and that he made his way from there to Jerusalem shortly before he prophesied. He must have been a very persuasive person, for in a brief space of about four months he was able to rouse the people of Jerusalem from their lethargy and to set them to rebuilding the Temple. He seems to have been one of the few prophets who was immediately successful in what he set out to accomplish. He was a man of one idea and one goal—the restoration of the house of the Lord.

Date and Background

Five dates are mentioned in the book (1:1,15; 2:1,10,20), all falling within the same year. According to 1:1, this was the second year of Darius, the Persian king, who ruled from 522 to 486 BC. Haggai's ministry, therefore, extended at least from September until December of 520 BC. During this brief period, he was able to rouse the Jewish community out of its lethargy and to set it to the task of rebuilding the Temple. According to Ezra 6:15, the task was completed four years later, in the sixth year of Darius.

Why had the returning exiles neglected to rebuild the Temple? A brief survey of the history of the period reveals that there were several reasons. They had returned from Babylon in 538 BC, about a year after Cyrus had conquered the Babylonians and set the captives free. Their leader was Sheshbazzar, described in Ezra 1:8 as "the prince of Judah." It has been suggested that he was the "Shenazzar" mentioned in 1 Chronicles 3:18, which would have made him the son of Jeconiah (Jehoiachin), the exiled king of Judah. Sheshbazzar had been appointed governor of the Persian province of Judah and had been authorized to rebuild the Jerusalem Temple on its ancient site (see Ezra 5:14-15).

Sheshbazzar did, indeed, lay the foundations of the Temple, but he was unable to bring it to completion (see Ezra 5:16). There were several factors that contributed to the suspension of the work. For one thing, the number of those who had returned from Exile was relatively small and the enormity of the task of rebuilding a ruined city taxed their meager resources. They decided that if they must choose between rebuilding the Temple and rebuilding houses to live in they would opt in favor of houses.

Another reason for the interruption in the work was the opposition of Judah's neighbors. The small community at Jerusalem was surrounded by Samaritans, Ashdodites, Ammonites, and Moabites. These spared no effort in trying to block the rebuilding of the Temple and succeeded in delaying it for almost twenty years (see Ezra 4:1-5,24).

During this interval, the returned exiles became more and more immersed in secular pursuits. The consolidation of Persia's control over their affairs caused them to despair of ever attaining political freedom or spiritual greatness.

In the meantime, Cyrus had died in 529 BC, to be succeeded by his son, Cambyses. Cambyses ruled until 522 BC at which time he died while on a campaign against Egypt. His death touched off a wave of revolt throughout the Persian Empire. Darius came to the throne at this critical juncture, and it took him about three years to restore order and regain control over the empire, as he himself told us in the Behistun Inscription.

By this time, Zerubbabel had been named as governor over the province of Judah; Joshua was named high priest. Zerubbabel is described as the son of Shealtiel (Hag. 1:1), thus making him the grandson of Jehoiachin, the exiled king of Judah (see 1 Chron. 3:17). Joshua the high priest was the son of Jehozadak (Hag. 1:1), who had been exiled to Babylon in 587 BC (see 1 Chron. 6:15).

It seems likely that Zerubbabel and Joshua arrived in Jerusalem early in 520 BC, bringing with them a fresh group of exiles from Babylon. Included in this group, in all probability, were the prophets Haggai and Zechariah. The fact that their arrival in Jerusalem came soon after the death of Cambyses and the subsequent rebellion that spread across the Persian Empire helps us to understand the note of expectancy that pervades the Books of Haggai and Zechariah. It also helps explain why Haggai pinned such high hopes on Zerubbabel, the heir of the house of David (see Hag. 2:23). It was a time when men and women dared dream of freedom and raise the hope that God was about to restore the kingdom to Israel.

Haggai seized upon this strategic moment in the history to convince the people that the time had come to raise up the Temple from its ruins. He was soon joined in this effort by the prophet Zechariah. The historian assigned to these two major credit for the completion of the Temple four years later (see Ezra 5:1-2; 6:14-15).

Message of the Book

The Temple played a vital role in the survival of the faith of Israel in the post-Exilic period. It served as a rallying point for Jews when many of them were scattered to the four corners of the earth. Without the Temple, it is doubtful that the religion of Israel could have survived the onslaughts of a pagan world. Judaism recognized its indebtedness to these two prophets who helped to make it a reality. Their hopes of freedom did not materialize, but they did lead a struggling community to rebuild its house of worship. And that was no small achievement.

Haggai has sometimes been criticized for appealing to the self-interest of the people as he sought to lead them to rebuild. He blamed their economic problems on their neglect of the Temple (Hag. 1:2-6) and promised prosperity if they would rebuild it (Hag. 2:6-9).

The answer to this criticism is that Haggai was addressing people who had become totally immersed in the search for the material to the exclusion of the spiritual. He was demanding of them nothing less than a total reorientation of their priorities.

This is an aspect of his preaching to which all of us need to give attention, for we too are prone to err in our allocation of priorities.

We usually find time and money for the things that really interest us. To say that we are too busy to serve God or too hard-pressed to support his work really says that he is not one of our priorities. The crucial question for each of us is this: to what is my life really committed? Haggai anticipated the words of our Lord, who said, "But seek first his kingdom and his righteousness, and all these things shall be yours as well" (Matt. 6:33).

An Urgent Appeal to Rebuild the Temple
1:1-11

Guilty by Reason of Negligence (1:1-6)

So far as we know, all of Haggai's ministry fell within the second year of Darius, king of Persia (520 BC). It began in the sixth month, corresponding to our August or September (see 1:1,15), was continued in the seventh month, corresponding to our October (see 2:1), and was concluded in the ninth month, corresponding to our December (see 2:10,18,20).

The people of Jerusalem justified their neglect of the Temple by saying that it was not the right time to undertake a building program (v. 2). Who has not heard this age-old excuse? It has been the refuge of timid souls in all generations. If we waited until all circumstances were favorable, we would never accomplish anything, either for ourselves or for the Lord. A wise man once said, "He who observes the wind will not sow;/and he who regards the clouds will not reap" (Eccl. 11:4). The real problem was that the people had grown accustomed to living in a city without a Temple and lacked the initiative to change the situation. Spiritual inertia can be a deadly disease. It is especially difficult to get people to undertake a given task when they have already tried it once and failed. They say, "That won't work here. We've already tried it once."

Haggai touched the heart of the problem when he charged the

people with putting their personal concerns before the concerns of God. They were unable to build the house of God and yet they found the time and the means to build paneled houses for themselves (v. 4). The prophet correctly diagnosed their problem as one of inverted priorities. They were placing first things last and last things first.

Haggai challenged the people to take stock of their situation (v. 5). Things had not worked out as they had anticipated. Keeping everything for themselves and giving nothing to God had not resulted in greater prosperity but in greater poverty (v. 6). There is no more telling description of the frustration of the self-centered life than that given here. The principle involved here is that economic well-being is closely related to spiritual well-being. This does not mean that the godly person will necessarily become prosperous, but it does mean that proserity cannot bring happiness to those who do not put God first in their lives.

A Plan for Bold Action (1:7-11)

The stones of the Temple laid where they had fallen. The people were to go up to the hills surrounding Jerusalem and gather wood and rebuild the Temple (vv. 7-8). To continue to neglect the Lord's house would only result in more of what they were already experiencing—drought and crop failure (vv. 9-11).

The calamities mentioned here are caused by what we normally refer to as "acts of nature," but which the insurance companies, curiously enough, still call "acts of God." To what extent are such occurrences "acts of God"? We know that some calamities, such as wars and famines, may result from humankind's misguided attempts to direct the affairs of life. But this does not adequately explain such natural occurrences as floods, droughts, tornadoes, and earthquakes. Are these perhaps also related to our inhumanity toward others, to our stupidity, and to our sinfulness? Is it too much to say that in a moral universe even nature itself is not neutral? Perhaps, in ways beyond our comprehension, there is a relationship between these violent eruptions of nature and the burden of human sin (see Rom. 8:19-23).

A Ready Response
1:12-17

Few prophets ever saw their preaching produce such quick results. The Lord stirred up the spirit of the leaders and of the people, and they were prepared to respond to the prophetic message. It is always easier to secure a response to our preaching when the Lord has gone before us.

This was a united response. It involved Zerubbabel, the governor; Joshua, the high priest; and all the remnant of the people (vv. 12,14). The verbs describing the response of the people reveal the quality of their commitment: they "obeyed the voice of the Lord their God" (v. 12a), they "feared before the Lord" (v. 12b), and "they came and worked on the house of the Lord" (v. 14). It is hard to defeat a congregation that demonstrates its commitment to the Lord through positive action. Verse 13 suggests that, as soon as the people made their response, Haggai changed his message from one of rebuke to one of encouragement.

The Greater Glory of the Second Temple
2:1-9

A crisis seems to have developed when the workers had been building about a month. As if it were not enough that the project was taxing their meager resources or that their neighbors were constantly harassing them, it slowly dawned on them that the Temple they were erecting fell far short of the splendor of that which it was meant to replace. In contrast to the Temple of Solomon, their Temple appeared to them as "nothing" (v. 3). Why go on building something that they would be ashamed of (see Ezra 3:12-13)? Why not abandon the effort altogether?

Haggai responded to the crisis with one of his most powerful sermons. It might well serve as a model for preachers today. He brought the word of God to bear upon a need that was felt and recognized by his listeners. He addressed them in such a manner that there was no doubt in their minds that his message was directed to them. His sermon was positive, relevant, and straightforward. Would that all preaching were like that!

The sermon gave a threefold charge to Zerubbabel, to Joshua, and to all the people of the land to "take courage" (v. 4). The literal meaning of this command is to be strong (see also Deut. 31:6,23; Josh. 1:9; Ps. 27:14). Two additional commands were given to reinforce the first. They were "work" (v. 4) and "fear not" (v. 5). "Take courage . . . work . . . fear not!"

Haggai's assurance to the embattled workers was rooted in his faith in God. He expressed this in three mighty words of hope.

(1) *Take courage for God is with you.* "For I am with you, says the Lord of hosts, according to the promise that I made you when you came out of Egypt. My Spirit abides among you; fear not" (vv. 4*b*-5; see also Ex. 3:12).

(2) *God is alive and active in the world.* "Once again, in a little while, I will shake the heavens and the earth and the sea and the dry land" (v. 6).

(3) *God has a glorious future for you and for this house.* First, he would cause the "treasures of all nations" (v. 7) to be brought so that his house would be filled with splendor. He could do this because he holds title to all the earth's silver and gold (v. 8).

The phrase translated "treasures of all nations" means literally "the choice things" or "the desirable things" of all nations. Jerome in the Vulgate translated this to read "the desired of all nations shall come" (see also the KJV). Certain Christian scholars then gave this a messianic interpretation, identifying "the desired of all nations" as Christ himself. This is a good example of how the plain meaning of a text may be altered through a mistranslation. The Old Testament has messianic passages, but this is not one of them.

Second, God promised that the latter splendor of this house would be greater than the former (v. 9*a*). In God's sight, the size and outward splendor of a sanctuary are not as important as the use that is made of it and the character of those who worship in it.

Third, God promised to bless his people with prosperity (v. 9*b*). The Hebrew for prosperity is *shalom,* one of the richest words in the vocabulary. Its root meaning is to be whole, complete, and finished.

It denotes a life of harmony, wholeness, success, prosperity, and well-being. It is the Old Testament equivalent of abundant living.

Promises of Better Things to Come
2:10-23

The Contagiousness of the Unclean (2:10-14)

On the twenty-fourth day of the ninth month (December) in the second year of Darius (520 BC), the prophet was instructed to seek from the priests a ruling (literally "a *torah*") on a difficult question (vv. 10-11). The question had to do with the relative contagiousness of holiness and uncleanness.

He first asked the priests if holiness were contagious to the touch, and their answer was, "No" (v. 12). Then he asked them if uncleanness were contagious to the touch, and their answer was, "Yes" (v. 13).

It is generally held that priests in Israel received answers to questions such as Haggai posed to them by casting the sacred lots, the Urim and the Thummim (see Ex. 28:30; Num. 27:21; 1 Sam 14:41; Ezra 2:63). The answer thus obtained, which was apparently limited to a yes or no, is called a *torah*. The Israelites believed that any answer obtained from the casting of lots was "wholly from the Lord" (Prov. 16:33).

Once Haggai had been told that uncleanness was contagious he applied this to his listeners. In some unexplained way, they had become unclean and, therefore, whatever they offered to the Lord was unclean (v. 14). The question that troubles the interpreter is the identity of the unclean group. Since they are called "this people" and "this nation" (v. 14), the prophet may have been saying that the Israelites had defiled themselves by neglecting to rebuild the Temple and that this defilement made it impossible for them to offer acceptable sacrifices to the Lord. Another suggestion is that the prophet may have been referring to the Samaritans as an unclean

people and warning the Israelites to have nothing to do with them.
Those who hold this view point out that the Samaritans asked to
have a part in rebuilding the Temple but were not permitted to do so
(see Ezra 4:1-5). The first suggestion sounds more convincing than
the second. If Haggai had wanted to warn against contacts with
foreigners, he could have done so in plain language.

A Forecast of Future Prosperity (2:15-19)

Haggai's forecast of future prosperity for the returned exiles is set
against a reminder of the bleak years that resulted from their
neglecting to rebuild the Temple of the Lord. However, the
reminder was not meant to discourage but to encourage.

The prophet asked them to remember how they fared before the
stones of the Temple began to be put in place (v. 15). Having set
themselves against God, they cut themselves off from the source of
every blessing. The Old Testament teaches that people are free to
choose by their actions whether they will expose themselves to
blessing or to disaster. When they choose to live lives of obedience
to God, their whole environment turns toward them with a friendly
face. However, if they choose to rebel, the same environment rises
up against them to destroy them (see Deut. 28). So long as the
people of Jerusalem neglected the Temple, they had nothing to
show for their toil except short yields (v. 16) and crop failures (v. 17).

Now, however, things were beginning to change. For three
months, from the twenty-fourth day of the sixth month (1:14-15) to
the twenty-fourth day of the ninth month (2:10,18), work had been
going forward on the rebuilding of the Temple. The prophet chose
this occasion to announce that empty barns would soon be filled
with grain and barren vineyards and orchards would again yield
their crops (vv. 18-19). The Lord's promise was sure: "From this day
on I will bless you."

The Shaking of the Heavens and the Earth (2:20-22)

In preparation for the restoration of his people, God announced
that he was about to shake the nations and to overthrow all warlike

powers (vv. 21-22). The shaking indicated here is like the shaking of an earthquake (see Pss. 46:3; 77:18; Amos 9:1). When the prophet delivered these words in 520 BC, he probably was thinking about the downfall of the Persian Empire and the establishment of God's rule over the nations. This oracle may have followed upon the news of fresh rebellions within the far-flung Persian Empire.

God's Plans for Zerubbabel (2:23)

Four words are addressed to Zerubbabel, and their significance is underscored by the fact that he was the grandson of King Jehoiachin (1:1; 1 Chron. 3:17) and, therefore, a descendant of the house of David.

First, the Lord told Zerubbabel that he would "take" him. This verb means to grasp firmly by the hand and is used in a figurative sense to describe the taking of a wife in marriage (see Gen. 4:19; 6:2; 11:29). In this sense, it means to take possession. It is also frequently used of God's choice of someone for a special mission, whether Abraham (Josh. 24:3) or all Israel (Ex. 6:7) or the Levites (Num. 3:12) or David (2 Sam. 7:8) or Amos (Amos 7:15). The word thus describes the establishing of a new relationship and the receiving of a new mission in life.

Next, the Lord called Zerubbabel "my servant." That this was meant as a title of honor is clear from its use elsewhere in the Old Testament, where it is applied to such persons as Abraham (Gen. 26:24), Moses (Ex. 14:31), and David (2 Sam. 3:18). Haggai may also have been influenced by its use in the Servant Songs in the latter part of the Book of Isaiah (see Isa. 42:1; 49:3,5-6; 52:13; 53:11). He may have looked upon Zerubbabel as in some sense the embodiment of the servant figure in these songs.

The Lord's third word to Zerubbabel was, I will "make you like a signet ring." This is an obvious reversal of the curse that Jeremiah had previously pronounced on Jehoiachin and all his descendants (see Jer. 22:24-30). Ancient rabbis taught that Jehoiachin later repented, and God reversed his sentence of doom on this account. A person's signet ring bore his own personal insignia and was used to sign letters and important documents (see 1 Kings 21:8). It was kept on the owner's person at all times, either fastened on a cord about the neck (see Gen. 38:18) or worn on one of the fingers of the right hand (see Jer. 22:24). For God to make Zerubbabel his signet ring meant that he was setting him up as his vice-regent on earth. He would be the earthly representative of the heavenly King.

The fourth word summed up all the others: "For I have chosen you, says the Lord of hosts." Haggai saw Zerubbabel as the chosen instrument of the Lord to bring about the downfall of the nations and to establish his rule on earth.

Some scholars think that these prophecies proved to be an embarrassment to Zerubbabel and led to his being removed from office by Darius. However, it is highly unlikely that Haggai's words would have been interpreted as advocating rebellion against Persia. He was more concerned with God's rule than with human efforts to regain independence. Ezra 6:13-15 implies that the Jews were able to complete the rebuilding of the Temple with the full support of the Persian officials.

ZECHARIAH

Introduction

The Prophet

The Book of Zechariah is perhaps the most underrated book in
the Old Testament. Early Christians placed great value on it, but in
our times it has suffered from neglect and misunderstanding.
Among the Minor Prophets, it is second in length only to the Book
of Hosea. However, in its grasp of the significance of the post-Exilic
period and of the purpose of God for the remnant of Israel, it is
second to none.

Zechariah was the son of Berechiah and the grandson of Iddo, the
prophet (1:1). According to Nehemiah 12:4, there was a man named
Iddo among the priests and Levites who returned to Jerusalem
under Zerubbabel around 520 BC. Assuming that Zechariah belonged to this man's family, it is likely that he arrived in Jerusalem at
this same time. This would also indicate that he had been born and
bred in a priestly family. Nehemiah 12:16 even informs us that
Zechariah had risen to become the head of the priests of the house
of Iddo during the high priesthood of Joiakim, the son of Joshua. His
priestly background helps us to understand his zeal for the rebuilding of the Temple and his concern for the purification of the
priesthood and of the land of Israel.

Date and Background

Haggai and Zechariah were contemporaries, and both were active
in urging the people to rebuild the Temple (Zech. 1:16-17; 4:9;
6:12-13; Ezra 5:1-2; 6:14-15). Haggai began to prophesy in the sixth
month of the second year of Darius (Hag. 1:1), and Zechariah joined
him in the eighth month of the same year (1:1). The ministry of
Zechariah lasted at least two years. One of his oracles is dated in the
fourth year of Darius (7:1). This means that he was active between

520 and 518 BC. Readers should consult the introduction to the Book of Haggai for a brief study of the historical background of this period.

The Book of Zechariah is divided into two main parts, the first consisting of chapters 1 to 8, and the second of chapters 9 to 14. It is widely held that the second part was written much later than the first and was among the last sections to be added to the prophetic canon.

The Message

Zechariah, like Haggai, was a promoter of the Temple. He went beyond Haggai, however, in sounding the prophetic call to repentance and to social righteousness (1:2-6; 7:8-14; 8:14-17). He said again that God's return to the Temple must be preceded by Israel's return to God (1:3).

A unique feature of Zechariah is the presentation of his message to the post-Exilic community through a series of eight visions (1:7-17; 1:18-21; 2:1-13; 3:1-10; 4:1-14; 5:1-4; 5:5-11; 6:1-8). The visions are somewhat like parables in that each one carries a central truth. This should caution us against giving undue attention to the minor details of the visions, many of which are obscure and have defied interpretation.

Zechariah is unique among the prophets in his attention to angels. In keeping with the post-Exilic concept of the transcendence of God, angels served as mediators between God and men. An angel interpreted God's revelations to the prophet and other angels carried out various missions for God (see 1:9-14; 2:3-5; 3:1-4; 4:1-7; 5:1-11; 6:1-8).

One of the heavenly beings who appears in the book is called literally "the Satan" (3:1-5), a title which means "the Accuser." It seems to have been his function to bring the failings of men to the attention of God. His role in Zechariah is much like that in the prologue to the Book of Job. It is only in 1 Chronicles 21:1 that Satan is written without an article and thus regarded as a proper name. The Chronicler is also the first to represent Satan as the instigator of sin. Zechariah's reference to Satan is the only such reference in the scroll of the prophets.

Although Zechariah taught by means of visions, he must not be regarded as a mere visionary. Through his visions, he was able to address some of the most pressing problems facing the post-Exilic community in Jerusalem. Those who had recently returned from Babylon faced obstacles that threatened their very existence. They were also filled with misgivings as to their relationship to God and as to his purpose for them. How did God intend to see them through this difficult moment in their history?

As Zechariah meditated on these complex problems, the solution to them came to him in a series of visions. The fact that the visions were given in the night (1:8) suggests that they may have had the form of dreams. Each vision addressed itself to a specific problem. Some of the most pressing problems were these: how would God fulfill his promises to restore Jerusalem in the face of the continuing dominance of the Persian Empire? Should Jerusalem be refortified? Was the high priest worthy of presiding over the Temple worship? What should be the relationship between the high priest and the governor? Would Zerubbabel be able to complete the rebuilding of the Temple? How could sin and guilt be removed from the land? How could the Jews still residing in Babylon be persuaded to return home and to participate in the rebuilding process?

Zechariah has been called the prophet of unrealized hopes. He appeared at a time when disappointment and disillusionment dogged the footsteps of the Jews. The burning hopes for freedom kindled by Darius' shaky beginning were soon doused as the king moved to consolidate his power. The band of exiles who had returned to Jerusalem was small and weak. The work of rebuilding the ruined Temple seemed slow and inconsequential, despite the able leadership of Zerubbabel and Joshua. Multitudes of Jews remained in Babylon, preferring the security that was assured there to the uncertainties of life in their ruined homeland.

The solution that Zechariah offered to his people was his profound belief that the rebuilding of Jerusalem and the Temple would usher in the messianic age and lead to the fulfillment of all their dreams. Even his name, which means "God remembers," was a symbol of his great faith. Zechariah's task was to quiet his people's fears about the state of the world, to inspire their zeal to rebuild, to restore their confidence in their leaders, and to assure them that God had forgiven their sin and was pleased to dwell once more in their midst.

A further word needs to be said about the messianic significance of the second part of the Book of Zechariah. Chapters 9 to 14 had special significance to the early disciples of Jesus. These chapters, together with the Suffering Servant passages in Isaiah and certain of the psalms, furnished the disciples with a biblical basis for understanding the crucifixion and death of Jesus.

The parallels begin when Jesus made his triumphal entry into Jerusalem, a scene that is described in all four of the Gospels. Zechariah 9:9 is quoted in Matthew 21:5 and in John 12:15. Matthew also connected Judas' thirty pieces of silver (Matt. 26:15; 27:3-10) and the wages paid to the unnamed shepherd (Zech. 11:12-13). Matthew 9:36 alludes to Zechariah 10:2 in its description of sheep without a shepherd. The scattering of the disciples at the time of Jesus' arrest (Matt. 26:31; Mark 14:27) is presented as a fulfilment of Zechariah 13:7. The pierced figure of Zechariah 12:10 is compared to Jesus in John 19:37 and in Revelation 1:7. These references give some notion of how the passion narratives in the Gospels are filled with quotations from Zechariah 9—14. It would be difficult to find such a collection of messianic texts anywhere else in the Old Testament.

First Section: Messages of Hope for Difficult Days
1:1 to 8:23

An Introductory Call to Repentance (1:1-6)

Zechariah's first message to the struggling community in Jerusalem in 520 BC was a call to repentance. The call was based on past experience. He reminded them of how the Lord had become angry with their fathers when they failed to heed his call to repentance delivered by the former prophets. He was doubtlessly thinking of such prophets as Hosea (Hos. 14:1-3), Amos (Amos 4:6-11), and Jeremiah (Jer. 25:5-7). A contrast is drawn in verses 5 and 6 between the precarious state of sinners and the permanence of the word of God. It is a word which pursues sinners until they are overtaken and destroyed. The stubborn refusal of the former generations to heed the word of God and the dire consequences that followed are also the subject of 7:8-14.

Eight Visions and Their Interpretations (1:7 to 6:8)

The First Vision: The Four Horsemen (1:7-17)

The vision (1:7-8).—The date mentioned in verse 7 (January/February, 519 BC) was the date when the prophet received all of his visions, not just the first one. There is an interesting parallel between this first vision and the last one described in 6:1-8, in that both involve horses and riders sent out to patrol the earth.

Its interpretation (1:9-11).—An accompanying angel furnished the prophet with an interpretation of his vision. When Darius became king, he established an Imperial Post, a kind of "Persian Pony Express," to improve communications between the various parts of his empire. Zechariah's visions of patrols riding on horses was probably influenced by this Persian innovation.

Some commentators, forgetting the parabolic nature of these visions, have tried to find allegorical meanings in all of their details. All such interpretations are highly subjective and unnecessary.

The key to the understanding of the first vision is found in verse 11, where those sent out to patrol the earth return to report: "We have patrolled the earth, and behold, all the earth remains at rest." In other words, the world situation had stabilized after the stormy period at the beginning of Darius's reign.

For the Jews, this was bad news. It meant an indefinite postponement to their hopes for freedom. Normally, for the land to be at rest was regarded as a good sign (see Judg. 3:11; 5:31; 8:28; 1 Kings 8:56; 2 Chron. 20:30; Isa. 14:7) but not under the circumstances in Zechariah's day. To be sure, Israel was at rest, but it was like a pigmy resting in the hands of a giant. It meant that Darius had put down all revolts and was firmly entrenched in power. It also meant that Haggai's expectations that the earth would soon be shaken and the nations destroyed as a prelude to Zion's glorification (see Hag. 2:6-9,20-23) had not come to pass.

Peace always means one thing to the oppressor and another to the oppressed. This is why it is sometimes difficult for us to understand what a nation like the Soviet Union means when it professes to be striving for peace. It often means no more than that she would like to see the downtrodden masses of Poland and Czechoslovakia accepting Communism in a peaceful way. Such a "peace" would be highly advantageous to her but disastrous to those whom she rules.

Lamentation over Jerusalem and the cities of Judah (1:12).—The angel of the Lord broke out into a lament over the unexpected and disappointing turn of events. The cry, "O Lord of hosts, how long" is familiar to us from the psalms of lament (see Pss. 13:2; 74:10; 79:5; 89:46). The subject of this lament is the apparent inactivity of God in the face of the continuing domination of Jerusalem by the Persians. Had not the Lord promised that Jerusalem's chastisement would last only seventy years (see Jer. 29:10-14)?

Seven words of consolation (1:13-17).—The Lord's response to the angel's lament consisted of seven reassuring words. (1) "I am exceedingly jealous for Jerusalem and for Zion" (v. 14*b*). This meant that the Lord had not forgotten his people (see Isa. 49:14-16). (2) "I am very angry with the nations that are at ease" (v. 15*a*). Being at ease refers to verse 11 and is meant as a characterization of the Persians. They were accused of having punished Israel more than the Lord intended that they should have been punished (see also Isa. 10:5-11; 47:6). (3) "I have returned to Jerusalem with compassion" (v. 16*a*). Ezekiel had predicted the Lord's departure from the city (Ezek. 11:22-23), but Zechariah was assured that God had returned. (4) "My house shall be built in it" (v. 16*b*; see also 4:8-10; 6:12-13,15). (5) "The measuring line shall be stretched out over Jerusalem" (v. 16*c*). This was a promise of the restoration of Jerusalem, whose future glory was painted in even sharper colors in 8:1-8,20-23. (6) "My cities shall again overflow with prosperity" (v. 17*a*; see also 2:4-5; 8:12-13). (7) "The Lord will again comfort Zion and again choose Jerusalem" (v. 17*b*; see also Isa. 40:1-2).

The Second Vision: The Four Horns and the Four Smiths (1:18-21)

This vision is also part of the Lord's response to the angel's lament in verse 12. The four horns represented all the heathen nations that had oppressed and scattered the people of God (v. 19*b*). The four smiths, or craftsmen, on the other hand, were sent to terrify and cast down the oppressing nations (v. 21).

There is calculated irony in four craftsmen terrifying an equal number of nations, especially when the list of nations included such giants as Assyria, Babylon, and Persia. The point of this passage is that the power of the nations would be broken not by soldiers armed with bow and spear and shield but by craftsmen armed with hammer and saw and plane. These were the very craftsmen who were engaged in rebuilding Jerusalem and its Temple (see v. 16). It was bold, indeed, for Zechariah to suggest that the ultimate downfall of all heathen powers was related to the zeal with which the men of Jerusalem drove nails and cut timbers to build the Temple.

The Third Vision: The Man with the Measuring Line (2:1-13)

Making preparations to measure Jerusalem (2:1-2).—The prophet saw a young man setting out to measure Jerusalem in order to establish its future boundaries. This may reflect an early attempt on the part of Zerubbabel to rebuild the walls of the city.

A city without walls (2:3-5).—An angel commanded the prophet to intercept the young man with the measuring line and to stop him from trying to measure the city. Two reasons were given for this action. First, so many persons would come to live in Jerusalem that its walls could not contain them. Second, the Lord himself would be a wall of fire about the city and a burning glory in its midst, and Jerusalem would have no need of other protection.

The concept of a city without walls was, indeed, a daring one. Walls served a twofold purpose in that they shut some in while shutting others out. Israel was not prepared to grasp Zechariah's concept of a city without walls. Nehemiah spoke a language they understood better when he called upon them to rebuild the walls.

It is doubtful that we understand this concept any better than they did, for consider the walls that we build. Our churches are hidden behind racial walls, creedal walls, and status walls. Some Christians feel we have raised walls to shut women out of ministry. We prefer a New Jerusalem, not without walls, but with strong walls all over the place. Have we forgotten that Jesus came to break down the walls that divide people (Eph. 2:14) and that in him our superficial distinctions mean nothing (Gal. 3:28)? We may persist in building walls, but our God will be just as persistent in breaking them down.

A summons to leave Babylon (2:6-13).—An urgent call went out for the remaining exiles to leave Babylon and to return to Jerusalem. Evidently there was a large community of Jews still residing in Babylon who showed no interest or enthusiasm for returning to Jerusalem. This oracle was directed to them.

Zechariah gave three good reasons they ought to return. First, God cared for them. According to ancient Jewish tradition the latter part of verse 8 should read: "For he who touches you touches the apple of my eye." To avoid such bold anthropomorphism, it was changed to read "his eye." "Apple of the eye" refers to the pupil of the eye, the most sensitive part of the eye and the part most carefully protected. Whoever touched the exiles had in effect put his finger in God's eye and could expect an immediate reaction from him. Second, God would soon plunder and destroy the nations among whom the exiles dwelled (vv. 6,9). Why should they cast their lot with nations that were doomed to destruction? Third, God would soon return to Zion and fill it with such glory that even the nations would seek to become a part of it (vv. 10-12; see also 8:20-23). How much more should the exiles desire to return so that they too might share in its glorious future. Many of the themes found in this section are present also in Isaiah 40—55.

The Fourth Vision: The High Priest in the Heavenly Court (3:1-10)

Satan's accusation against Joshua (3:1).—The fourth and fifth visions deal with the character and relationship of Joshua and Zerubbabel, the divinely appointed leaders of the post-Exilic community. The fourth vision suggests that there were those in Jerusalem who challenged Joshua's fitness to serve as high priest in the restored Temple. Perhaps it was because he had just returned from Babylon and was regarded as unclean by reason of having resided in a foreign land. Or perhaps all the priests were regarded as still contaminated by the guilt that led to the destruction of Solomon's Temple in 587 BC.

Satan has the article in the Hebrew of verse 1, indicating that it is a title, perhaps best translated as "the Accuser." Here, as in the opening chapters of Job, his role was to challenge the worthiness of God's servants and to question the authenticity of thir piety.

The Lord's rebuke of Satan (3:2).—The Lord halted Satan before he could make an accusation against Joshua and reminded Satan that Joshua, perhaps symbolizing all the inhabitants of Jerusalem, was like "a brand plucked from the fire" (v. 2; see also Amos 4:11). This was a proverbial way of speaking of a miraculous escape.

Joshua vindicated (3:3-5).—Joshua was represented as standing in the heavenly court clothed in filthy garments, symbolizing the doubts that had been raised as to his worthiness to function as high priest. The angel then commanded that the filthy garments should be removed and that he should be clothed with rich apparel and that a clean turban should be placed on his head. The Christian reader is reminded of similar orders given by the father whose prodigal son had returned from a far country (see Luke 15:20-24).

Joshua granted access to the heavenly court (3:6-7).—The angel of the Lord promised Joshua access to the heavenly court provided he walked in God's ways and kept his charge. Access to God's heavenly court was a privilege granted only to the prophets in the pre-Exilic period (see Jer. 23;18,22), which made it all the more significant that it should be extended to the high priest. To be granted access to the heavenly temple should have removed all doubts as to his worthiness to enter the earthly Temple.

Messianic promises (3:8-10).—There is a cluster of messianic sayings at the end of the fourth vision. Verse 8 contains two such sayings. The first describes Joshua and his fellow priests as a sign or an omen. There is no adjective in the Hebrew. Whether an omen is good or bad depends upon the context. In most of its uses in the Old Testament, it serves notice of an approaching calamity. As Zechariah used it, however, it means that the restored priesthood was an omen of the advent of the Messiah, a promise and a prophecy of the messianic kingdom soon to be established.

The second saying in verse 8 has to do with the coming of one who is called "my servant the Branch." A preferable translation would be "the Shoot" since the word stands for that which shoots up or sprouts out of the earth. Even before Zechariah appeared on the scene, this word had become a metaphor for the long-awaited Messiah (see Isa. 4:2; Jer. 23:5; 33:15). It is apparent that Zechariah interpreted the Branch as Zerubbabel since in 4:9 he insisted that Zerubbabel would complete the Temple and in 6:12-13 attributed the success of that venture to one called "the Branch."

The significance of the joining together of these two sayings in verse 8 should not be overlooked. With the Temple finished and with Joshua as high priest and Zerubbabel as ruler, Zechariah

thought the restoration of Israel would be complete (see also Hag.
2:23).

It is possible that the stone set before Joshua (v. 9) was a further
reference to Zerubbabel, especially since he also appeared in 4:10
with a "measuring stone" or "plummet" in his hand, the Hebrew
word being the same in both instances. However, it seems more
likely in the light of a similar passage in Isaiah 28:16 that the stone of
verse 9 refers to the keystone, or capstone, of the Temple, that
wedge-shaped piece at the summit of an arch which held the other
pieces in place. The stone which Zechariah saw had seven facets,
each of which bore an inscription, also in the manner of the stone in
Isaiah 28:16. It is possible that there were seven identical inscriptions, one on each of the seven facets of the stone. What the
inscriptions said is not clear, although there is a clue to the contents
at the end of verse 9: "I will remove the guilt of this land in a single
day." It must have contained an assurance from the Lord that there
would be full and final forgiveness for Israel on the day when the
final stone was placed in the Temple.

Verse 10 promised that, when the messianic day dawned, every
Israelite would play host to his neighbor "under his vine and under
his fig tree." While this might draw upon a similar promise in Micah
4:4, it is even more closely related to 1 Kings 4:25, which affirms that
throughout the reign of Solomon all of the Israelites from Dan to
Beersheba dwelt in safety, "every man under his vine and under his
fig tree." It is surely no accident that Zechariah expected the
peaceful conditions of Solomon's reign to return when the Temple of
Solomon had been restored.

The Fifth Vision: The Lampstand and the Olive Trees (4:1-14)

The vision given (4:1-5).—Strong opposition to Zerubbabel's
leadership seems to have developed in the Jerusalem community.
His critics leveled two charges at him: (1) that he and Joshua had not
been chosen by the Lord to lead the community, and (2) that
because of this he would not be able to complete the rebuilding of
the Temple. Even Zechariah seems to have come under fire for his
strong support of these two leaders, his critics charging that the
Lord had not sent him to prophesy to them. The purpose behind the
vision and the words of encouragement to Zerubbabel in chapter 4 is
to show that he and Joshua stood in the closest possible relationship
to the Lord, that he would be successful in completing the Temple,

and that his success would prove that Zechariah was a true prophet of the Lord.

The prophet apparently received the vision while sleeping, after which he was awakened by an angel and asked to describe what he had seen (v. 1). His answer revealed that he had seen a golden lampstand (Hebrew: *menorah*) with seven lamps. There was a bowl above the lampstand, the apparent purpose of which was to supply oil to the lamps. He also saw two olive trees standing beside the lampstand, one on either side. He did not readily perceive the meaning of the vision and asked the angel to explain it to him.

Words of encouragement to Zerubbabel (4:6-10a).—Instead of giving an interpretation of the vision, this section provides a message of encouragement to Zerubbabel. The vision is interpreted in verses 10b-14. There is some question as to whether the chapter has been preserved in its original order (see the footnote in the GNB).

The first word to Zerubbabel was both a word of warning and a word of encouragement: "Not by might, or by power, but by my Spirit, says the Lord of Hosts" (v. 6b). It was a word of warning, lest either he or the people of Jerusalem think of the Temple as a product of their own effort and ingenuity. It was also a word of encouragement, for he was assured that he would be able to complete a task for which his own resources were totally inadequate. The purpose of this promise was not to discourage human effort, as if all Zerubbabel had to do was fold his hands and wait for God to work a miracle. Rather, the promise reminds us that our greatest achievements are those in which God takes us beyond the limits of our own resources and replaces our spent power with his spiritual power.

Verse 7 opens with a rebuke addressed to the mountain that stood in Zerubbabel's way. The mountain symbolized all of the obstacles that he had to overcome in order to complete the Temple. The verse ends with a promise that the mountain would become a plain before Zerubbabel and that he would set the top stone of the Temple in place on a day of shouting and singing.

Verses 9 and 10 repeat the divine affirmation that Zerubbabel would achieve success, thus putting to silence all his critics. His hands laid the foundations of the Temple, and those same hands would put the finishing touches to it (v. 9a). When this had occurred, all Israel would know that the Lord had indeed sent Zechariah to be the prophet of those things (v. 9b). Verse 10a is a word of rebuke and also a word of promise. It was addressed to the skeptics within the community who had "despised the day of small things," an apparent reference to their apathy toward the Temple and their disappointment in its appearance as compared to Solomon's Temple (see Hag. 2:3; Ezra 3:12). Their skepticism would soon turn to rejoicing when they saw Zerubbabel ascending to the pinnacle of the Temple with plummet in hand in order to set the top stone in place (see also 3:9; 4:7).

The vision interpreted (4:10b-14).—The vision given in verses 1-5 was then interpreted. The seven lamps on the golden lampstand represented the eyes of the Lord (v. 10b). Seven is the number of completion. Its use here symbolized the Lord's ever-present watchfulness over his people.

The two olive trees represented Zerubbabel and Joshua, who stood in the presence of the Lord and who shared the responsibility for directing the affairs of the community (v. 14; see also 6:12-13). Some interpret verse 12 as meaning that the oil for the lamps came from the two olive trees, but in order to arrive at such an interpretation they have to make the lampstand a symbol for the restored Jewish community, which drew its strength from its political and religious leaders. Not to change the symbolism of the lampstand would make the Lord himself dependent upon the two leaders, an absurd situation. The problem can be avoided simply by accepting the interpretation that the passage itself gives for the vision. It clearly states that the seven lamps on the lampstand are the eyes of the Lord (v. 10b) and that the two olive trees are the two anointed leaders who stood always in the Lord's presence (v. 14). The vision thus interpreted was a powerful rebuke to those who would challenge the leaders' credentials.

The Sixth Vision: The Flying Scroll (5:1-4)

The vision (5:1-2).—Zechariah saw a flying scroll, measuring twenty by ten cubits, or approximately thirty by fifteen feet.

Its interpretation (5:3-4).—The scroll was inscribed with the curse of the Lord against sinners, reminding us of the curses of Deuteronomy 27:15-26 and 28:15-68.

The flying scroll was patrolling the skies over the land of Judah, ready to descend upon the houses of evildoers, much like the death angel descended upon the houses of the Egyptians (Ex. 12:12-13,23).

Two forms of wickedness, stealing and false swearing, are singled out for special condemnation, although they may have been intended as representative of all wickedness. If anyone had committed either of these sins, the flying curse would come down upon his house and abide there until that house was wiped out. This must have been a stern warning to any who might have thought that the Lord had relaxed his requirements for personal righteousness in the post-Exilic period.

The Seventh Vision: The Flying Barrel (5:5-11)

The vision (5:5-6a).—Zechariah saw a barrel (see NEB; RSV has "ephah") about ready to take off on a flight from the land of Judah. Like the preceding vision, this one was concerned with the removal of evil from the land as a prelude to the coming of the messianic age.

Its interpretation (5:6b-8).—The lead covering of the barrel was momentarily lifted and the prophet saw a woman seated inside it. He was told that she personified all the iniquity and wickedness in the land (vv. 6b,8a). No special significance attaches to the fact that wickedness is personified as a woman, except that the Hebrew word for *wickedness* has the feminine form. As the covering was lifted, the woman tried to escape but was quickly thrust back inside the barrel and the lid was shut.

The removal of the barrel to the land of Shinar (5:9-11).—Two women came forward, having wings like a stork. They lifted up the barrel containing wickedness and flew with it to Shinar, the ancient name for Babylon (see Gen. 11:2; Isa. 11:11). There a temple was erected to house the barrel and its sinister cargo and worship was offered to it. This was definitely a polemic against pagan religion. It probably reflected the view of the Jews of the post-Exilic period that only in Jerusalem could true worship be offered to the Lord. This vision set the stage for the eighth and final vision.

The Eighth Vision: The Four Chariots (6:1-8)

The vision (6:1-3).—The eighth vision shared many of the features of the first vision (1:7-17). Both involved horses. The horses had riders in the first vision but pulled chariots in this one. In each instance their task was to patrol the earth and to report to the Lord.

Its interpretation (6:4-8).—We must be especially careful to observe the parabolic nature of a vision such as this, resisting the temptation to search for allegorical meaning in its various details. Verses 4-5 suggest a setting for the vision in the heavenly council, where the messengers of God came to present their reports after fanning out through the earth (see Job 1:6-7; 2:1-2).

Zechariah saw the chariots and their riders being sent out to patrol the earth. It soon became evident that their primary mission was toward the "north country," an apparent reference to Babylon. At the end of their patrol, the Lord reported to Zechariah, "Behold, those who go toward the north country have set my Spirit at rest in the north country." This is obviously the key to the meaning of the vision, although it lends itself to several interpretations. One is that the remaining exiles had been persuaded to return from the north country. A more likely interpretation is that punishment had been inflicted upon Babylon, the destroyer of the Temple and the oppressor of God's people, thereby setting God's Spirit at rest in the north country.

The Crowning of Joshua (6:9-15)

This passage treats the crowning of the messianic ruler, who in verse 11 is identified as Joshua the high priest. However, there is strong evidence that the passage originally referred to the crowning of Zerubbabel or at least to a dual ceremony in which both he and Joshua were crowned, the Hebrew word for crown appearing twice in the passage and always in the plural form (vv. 11,14). Evidence that Zerubbabel was the original recipient of the crown is found in the bestowal speech in verses 12-13, which uses terminology that is elsewhere unmistakably applied to him (see 3:8; 4:8-10). It is possible that the name of Zerubbabel was deleted from the text when the hopes connected with him failed to materialize and when it became evident that the high priest was the only Jewish authority left with any vestige of power. Passages such as this contributed to the later Jewish expectation that there would be two Messiahs, one from the house of David and one from the house of Levi.

The Making of the Crown (6:9-11)

The crown (or crowns) was made from gold and silver contributed by some exiles who had recently arrived in Jerusalem from Babylon (vv. 10-11). There is disagreement in the names of the exiles as given in verses 10 and 14. This is further complicated by the Septuagint, which has only one name in the list of returnees in verse 10, namely that of Joshua the son of Zephaniah. There is no satisfactory solution to this problem.

The Successful Mission of the Branch (6:12-13)

In an address perhaps originally intended for Zerubbabel, it was said that one called the Shoot would shoot up (thus preserving the play on words of the Hebrew) in his place, that he would complete the building of the Temple, and that he would rule upon his throne. In an apparent reference to the relationship that the Lord purposed should exist between Joshua and Zerubbabel, it was said that the king should have a priest beside his throne and that there should be peaceful understanding between the two (v. 13; see also 4:12-14).

The Placing of the Crown in the Temple (6:14)

After the coronation ceremony had been concluded, the crown was to be deposited in the Temple, much like the British crown jewels are kept in the Tower of London. I think that, when Zerubbabel proved not to be the awaited messianic prince, the crown was laid up in the Temple to await the coming of the true Messiah.

Reinforcements for Rebuilding the Temple (6:15)

This verse furnishes evidence that Zechariahs' visions were given sometime before the Temple was completed. It announced that a fresh band of exiles would come to assist in the rebuilding of the Temple. An appeal to the exiles to join in this undertaking had been issued in 2:6-7.

The Essence of True Religion (7:1-14)

Sometime around November, 518 BC, while the building of the Temple was still in progress, a delegation from Bethel in the former territory of the Northern Kingdom came to Jerusalem to ask the priests and prophets if they were free to discontinue a fast that they had been observing for a number of years. It was the fast of the fifth month, the fast held in commemoration of the burning of the

Temple in 587 BC (2 Kings 25:8-9; Jer. 52:12-13). Since the house of the Lord was being rebuilt, perhaps it was time to discontinue that fast.

The passage does not indicate what answer was given to the delegates from Bethel. Zechariah, who must have been among the prophets consulted, addressed his words to all the people of the land and especially to the priests. He used the occasion to deliver a sermon on the limited value of all fasting and on the essence of true religion.

The Dubious Value of Fasting (7:1-6)

The subject of fasting seems to have been a live issue in the post-Exilic period (see Isa. 58:3-12). The only fast mentioned in the Pentateuch is on the Day of Atonement (see Lev. 16:29-31; Num. 29:7,12), but four additional fasts were added after the Exile. They were held in commemoration of the day the seige of Jerusalem began, the day it fell, the day the Temple was burned, and the day that Gedaliah was murdered (see 7:5; 8:19).

Fasting was a form of self-humiliation involving abstention from food and drink for a prescribed period of time. Its purpose was to focus the attention of worshipers on their spiritual rather than their physical needs and to call God's attention to their desperate plight (see 1 Sam. 7:6; 31:13; Joel 1:14; 2:15-16).

Zechariah stressed the dubious value of fasting. His words in verses 5-6 suggest that neither fasting nor feasting has any value beyond that which it has for the one engaged in it. In other words, there is no inherent religious value in either.

God's Unyielding Demand for Justice and Obedience (7:7-14)

The essence of true religion does not lie in observing fasts or religious festivals but in rendering true judgments, in showing kindness and mercy toward one's brother, in protecting the helpless members of the community, and in taking care not to devise evil against others (vv. 9-10). Zechariah defined the requirements of religion very much in the spirit of Amos, who also warned against substituting religious observances for the kindness and compassion that should be shown toward others (see Amos 5:21-24).

Zechariah stressed that these had always constituted God's demands upon Israel, as communicated to her through the former prophets (v. 7). He also warned that it was Israel's ignoring of these demands that led to her downfall (vv. 11-14). Let the post-Exilic community take heed lest it too forfeit its future hope through disobedience.

Ten Promises for a Bright Future (8:1-23)

The Promise of God's Unfailing Zeal for His People (8:1-2)

This promise is almost identical to that given in 1:14-15. It expresses God's unfailing watchcare over his people and his wrath toward all who would oppress them.

The Promise of God's Transforming Presence in Jerusalem (8:3)

This promise is also a repetition of that given in 1:16. God promised to return to Zion (see Ezek. 43:1-5) and to take up his dwelling place in Jerusalem. The word to dwell means to pitch one's tent or to make camp in a certain place. The same word in its Greek form appears in John 1:14, where it describes God's tabernacling among us in the person of Jesus Christ. This Hebrew verb gave rise to the noun *Shekinah*, which also expresses God's presence with his people.

The Promise of the Joyful Intermingling of Young and Old in the Streets of Jerusalem (8:4-5)

Again this promise should be compared to that given in 1:17, both of which refer to the welfare of the cities of Judah in the messianic age. Zechariah promised that, when the Lord took up his dwelling place in Jerusalem, the streets of the city would become a playground for little boys and girls and safe resting place for old men and women. The view that the play of children is important to God is both interesting and refreshing. Equally interesting is the view that old age is not eliminated in the messianic age but transformed into a time of peaceful contentment and security.

The Promise That the Lord Is Unimpressed by Difficult Tasks (8:6)

The simple statement of this verse is that while some things may be "marvelous" in the eyes of men, they never seem "marvelous" to

God. Elsewhere in the Old Testament this verb means to be difficult
or to appear to be impossible (see Gen. 18:14; Deut. 17:8; 2 Sam.
13:2; Jer. 32:17,27). This verse has reference to the obstacles that lay
in the way of the rebuilding of the Temple and the inauguration of
the messianic age.

The Promise of the Ingathering of the Exiles and the Renewal of the Covenant Relationship (8:7-8)

Earlier God had promised that he would dwell in the midst of
Jerusalem (v. 3). Now he promised that the exiles would be gathered
from the ends of the earth in order that they too may dwell in the
midst of Jerusalem (vv. 7-8). The peaceful coexistence of God and his
people implied the renewal of the covenant. This was expressed in
language reminiscent of Hosea: "And they shall be my people and I
will be their God, in faithfulness and in righteousness" (see Hos.
2:19-20,23).

The Promise of the Completion of the Temple and the Restoring of Prosperity and Dignity to Judah (8:9-13)

This section begins and ends with an exhortation addressed to
those who responded to the call of the prophets and began to
rebuild the Temple: "Let your hands be strong." They were reminded of the widespread unemployment and violence that filled
the land before they began their work (v. 10). They were also
promised that the completion of their work would produce a sowing
of peace and prosperity in the land (v. 12). The description of the
farmer sowing seeds of peace is powerful symbolism, for there can
be no lasting peace in the world so long as two thirds of its
population go hungry. The return of prosperity would also mark the
return of dignity to Judah. She would no longer be a byword of
cursing among the nations, but a source of blessing (v. 13). This is an
obvious reference to the promise made to Abraham in Genesis
12:2-3.

The Promise of Unfailing Blessing for an Obedient People (8:14-17)

Promise and demand meet in these verses. Judah was reminded
that God adheres to his declared purpose, whether it be to punish
rebellion, as in the case of their fathers (v. 14), or to reward
obedience (v. 15). They would assuredly be blessed if they became
an obedient people.

What this means in practical terms was clearly stated in verses 16-17. These were God's demands for a better world. They could be summed up in one demand, the demand for truth (v. 16). God, who is a God of truth (Isa. 65:16), desires truth as the controlling force in the lives of his followers (Ps. 51:6). Therefore he hates duplicity, lying, and false swearing (v. 16).

Truth and peace are shown by this verse to be interrelated (see also Jer. 33:6 in its Hebrew form), just as food and peace were shown in verse 12 to be related. Even as there can be no lasting peace where people are starving, so there can be no enduring peace where human relations are governed by lies and falsehood. How simple are God's demands for a better world, and yet how difficult to attain!

The Promise of the Transformation of Fasts into Feasts (8:18-19)

Zechariah apparently felt that fasting was out of place in the new age that was dawning with the rebuilding of the Temple. The dominant note in the new age was not to be one of gloom but of celebration. Therefore, the four fasts, commemorating the beginning of the seige of Jerusalem (see 2 Kings 25:1; Jer. 52:4), the breaching of the walls of the city (see 2 Kings 23:3-5), the burning of the city and the Temple (see Jer. 52:12-13), and the assassination of Gedaliah (see 2 Kings 25:23,25; Jer. 41:1-3), were to be transformed into seasons of joy and gladness (v. 19). Instead of fasting, the worshipers would spend these days feasting. It would be difficult to imagine a more complete transformation than that envisioned here.

The Promise of a Worldwide Pilgrimage to Jerusalem (8:20-22)

The thrust of these verses is that Gentiles would come from all parts of the earth in order to entreat the favor of the Lord in Jerusalem (see also Isa. 2:2-4; 18:7; 19:19-25; 60:1-7; 61:5-6; Zech. 14:16).

The Promise of the Attraction of the Gentiles to the God of the Jews (8:23)

This tenth promise is an extension of the ninth. In applying the promise to our day and situation, we might note that there are two ways in which the world's lost are persuaded to turn to God for salvation. One is by being drawn to a body of believers and asking to share their faith. The other is by hearing the gospel proclaimed by missionaries sent out to evangelize.

The first way might be called centripetal, which means proceeding to or directed toward the center. It implies a body of believers so committed to the Lord that others are naturally drawn to them. The other way would be called centrifugal, moving or directed outward from the center. It involves a body of believers committed to support for and involvement in the missionary task.

In the Old Testament, Israel's responsibility toward the nations is described in centripetal terms. Israel was to live in such a vital relationship to the Lord that the nations would be drawn to her and would ask to participate in her religion. She would not need to seek them, for they would seek her. In the words of this verse, "Ten men from the nations of every tongue shall take hold of the robe of a Jew saying, 'Let us go with you, for we have heard that God is with you'" (see also 9:16; Isa. 2:2-4).

The emphasis changes somewhat in the New Testament. The Christian churches are not to neglect the cultivation of a strong and dedicated membership, else they will forfeit their very right to exist. At the same time, they are to organize missionary efforts to reach the lost, beginning near at home and continuing to the ends of the earth (see Acts 1:8). *Being* and *going* are the two most important words in the church's vocabulary.

This verse (v. 23) should also remind us that the only excuse the Christian has for seeking to exert influence over others is that they might be led to God. We are not the apostles of a particular social or economic system, whether we serve at home or overseas. Rather, we were placed in the world in order that we might make friends for God.

Second Section: The Glories of the Messianic Age
9:1 to 14:21

The Book of Zechariah changes completely when one passes from chapters 1—8 to 9—14. In the first section the materials are carefully dated, but there are no dates given in the second section. All references to Zechariah, Joshua, and Zerubbabel are also limited to the first section. The interpreting angel, mentioned often in 1—8, drops out of sight in 9—14. The Temple, so prominent in 1—8, is not even alluded to in 9—14. In literary form and style, there is also a marked difference between the two sections, 1—8 being presented in the form of visions and 9—14 in the form of apocalyptic discourses. The historical situation is also different. The nations are at rest in 1—8, but in 9—14 they are in commotion and threatening the very existence of Jerusalem. The Persians have also passed off the scene, and their place has been taken by the Greeks (see 9:13).

There is no easy solution to the problem of date and authorship of the final chapters of the book. Matthew 27:9, quoting Zechariah 11:13, seems to assign them to Jeremiah. A more likely date would be around 300 BC, after the conquests of Alexander the Great. However, there are some who would place them in the sixth century BC, in the same period as chapters 1—8.

The First Oracle: Preparations for the Messianic Age (9:1 to 11:17)

The latter part of Zechariah is divided into two sections of more or less equal length and each bearing in Hebrew the heading "Oracle [or burden] of the word of the Lord" (see 9:1 and 12:1). The same heading appears at the beginning of Malachi, which has led some to propose that these were three collections that circulated independently before they were affixed to the end of the Minor Prophets.

The Lord's Victory Over the Nations (9:1-8)

These verses describe the impending judgment of the Lord upon the cities of Syria, Phoenicia, and Philistia. The instrument the Lord used to devastate these cities is not named, but most commentators take it to be Alexander the Great, mainly because of the reference to the destruction of Tyre (vv. 2-4). It is known that Alexander destroyed the city in 332 BC, after a seige of seven months.

Of special interest was the announcement that the survivors from among the Philistines would abstain from eating blood and other abominable foods condemned in the Law (v. 7a; see also Gen. 9:4; Lev. 17:10-14; Deut. 14:3-20). Furthermore, they would become a remnant for God, being counted as one of the clans of Judah and being incorporated into the nation like the ancient Jebusites (v. 7*b*). Over this expanded realm the messianic King would come to rule (vv. 9-10).

The Triumphal Entry of Zion's King (9:9-10)

These verses celebrate the coming of the messianic Prince to Jerusalem. They are especially familiar to Christian readers because of their use in the New Testament to describe Jesus' triumphal entry into Jerusalem on Palm Sunday (see Matt. 21:5; John 12:15). Even ancient Jewish scholars interpreted these verses in a messianic sense.

In preparation for his coronation, the messianic Prince would ride into Jerusalem amid shouts of joy and rejoicing. His representation in these verses is based in part upon the mysterious figure set forth in Genesis 49:10-12 and in part upon the description of Solomon's coronation in 1 Kings 1:38-40.

The messianic Prince would come in triumph. The Hebrew suggests that he would enter the gates of the city as the recipient of salvation and victory (see also Ps. 118:25-26). He is also called "humble," an adjective that elsewhere means "lowly," "poor," and "afflicted." The same Greek word is used to translate this adjective as appears in the third Beatitude in Matthew 5:5. The composite portrait thus afforded resembles both the ideal king and conquering hero of Isaiah 9:2-7 and the Suffering Servant of Isaiah 52:13 to 53:12. The difficulty of combining these two concepts finally led the Jews to assume two Messiahs, a son of Joseph who by his death would provide atonement and expiation for sin and a son of David who would follow him and rule in glory and splendor. Christians believe these two concepts were fused in Jesus of Nazareth, who was both conquering King and Suffering Servant.

Jerusalem's Messiah also entered as a champion of peace, which is symbolized by his riding upon an ass. The ass or mule was traditionally used as a royal steed, and to ride upon one was in no sense demeaning (see Judg. 5:10; 10:4; 12:14; 1 Sam. 25:20; 2 Sam. 13:29; 18:9; 1 Kings 1:38; 18:5). It is true, however, that when kings came as warriors they rode upon horses (see 1 Kings 20:20; Prov. 21:31; Jer. 8:16; Ezek. 23:23; Zech. 10:5). The ass is used in this passage, therefore, not as a symbol of lowliness but of peaceful intent. Throughout the messianic passages in the Old Testament, there is a strong emphasis on peace (see Isa. 2:2-4; 9:2-7; 11:6-9; Mic. 5:2-5). According to verse 10, the messianic King would banish the chariot from Ephraim (Northern Israel) and the war horse from Jerusalem (Judah). This implies a united kingdom that would have no further need for a standing army since Messiah himself would be its strong defender. He would command peace to the nations and his rule would extend to the ends of the earth.

The Glorious Future of God's Flock (9:11-17)

The militant spirit of this passage contrasts sharply with the preceding verses. It opens with a declaration of the Lord's intent to free the captives from their prison dungeon (v. 11). They were set and commanded to return to their stronghold, that is, to Jerusalem (v. 12). The Lord himself would fight beside them and enable them to inflict upon their enemies a crushing defeat (vv. 13-15). The Greeks were the victims of the Lord's wrath in this wild and bloody battle scene (v. 13). Who, except a Hebrew prophet, would have dared believe that the tiny kingdom of Judah would outlast the mighty Greek empire!

As this passage comes to a close, the storm clouds break and the sun shines through. Leaving behind the battlefield with its blood and gore, we find ourselves on a quiet hillside where a shepherd tended his flock. The shepherd is the Lord and the sheep are his people. They shine on his land like jewels on a crown (v. 16*b*), a reference to the grassy green hillsides of Palestine dotted with flocks of white sheep. The messianic age will also be a time of great prosperity, with the land yielding an abundance of grain and new wine (v. 17; see also Hos. 2:21-22; Amos 9:13-15).

The Lord of the Weather (10:1-2)

Continuing the theme of the land and its produce, Israel was reminded that the enriching rains came from the Lord (v. 1) and not from the teraphim (v. 2; see also 2 Kings 23:24; Hos. 3:4). To turn from the Lord to worthless idols was to follow a delusion and to become like sheep without a shepherd (v. 2). Israel's God was Lord of history and also Lord of creation.

The Lord's Care for His Flock (10:3-5)

While it is bad to have sheep without a shepherd (v. 2*b*), it is even worse to have shepherds who do not care for the sheep. Such were the shepherds, or foreign rulers, who were oppressing the flock of God (v. 3a). Soon God would turn the tables on the cruel shepherds and transform the emaciated sheep into mighty war horses (v. 3b), who would then turn on the shepherds and trample them into the mire of the streets (v. 5). From the flock itself God would raise up leaders who would be the foundation, support, and protection of his people (v. 4).

The Ingathering of Judah and Israel (10:6 to 11:3)

The ingathering of the scattered exiles from Judah (the Southern Kingdom) and from Joseph (the Northern Kingdom) is treated in verses 6-10. What is clearly indicated here is the reunion of the kingdom and its restoration to its former glory. Even the territory of Gilead and Lebanon would be included in the restored kingdom (v. 10). God would have compassion on them and treat them as though they had never been unfaithful (v. 6). They would fill up the land as in days of old (vv. 8b,10b), and would become a strong and happy people (v. 7).

Their former enemies would not be so fortunate. Their overthrow is predicted in 10:11 to 11:3. Verses 11 and 12 have textual problems, but as rendered in *The New English Bible* they read:

> Dire distress shall come upon the Euphrates
> and shall beat down its turbulent waters;
> all the depths of the Nile shall run dry.
> The pride of Assyria shall be brought down,
> and the sceptre of Egypt shall pass away;
> but Israel's strength shall be in the Lord,
> and they shall march proudly in his name.
> This is the very word of the Lord.

Lebanon and Bashan, known for their tall and stately trees, are made to represent all the powers that have oppressed Israel (11:1-2). Their mighty forests would be felled and burned with fire. Their kings, described first as shepherds and then as lions, would roar and wail when their habitations are destroyed (v. 3). The sound of joy went up from the kingdom of Israel (10:7), the sound of distress from the kingdoms of the nations (11:1-3).

The Allegory of the Rejected Shepherd (11:4-17)

It seems that this allegory was designed to speak to the crisis of leadership in the post-Exilic period. It speaks of good leaders (good shepherds) and bad leaders (bad shepherds) and suggests that in some sense the people (the sheep) had been free to choose which type of shepherd would rule over them. Because they had despised and rejected the good shepherd whom God had set over them (vv. 4-14), they were delivered over to a worthless shepherd who cared nothing for them (vv. 15-17). This stress upon the stubborn behavior of the people and the reaction of God has led one commentator to entitle the section, "God's Judgment upon an Ungrateful People."

God commanded the prophet to become the shepherd of a flock here described as "doomed to slaughter" (vv. 4,7). The reason for their plight was that they had fallen into the hands of shepherds interested only in exploiting them for what they would bring in the marketplace or at the slaughterhouse (vv. 5,7,11). Bible students debate whether this refers to foreign kings who were oppressing the Israelites or to local leaders who were exploiting their own people. It is possible that both groups were included in the Lord's indictment.

The prophet obeyed the Lord's command and assumed the role of the good shepherd, tending his flock with gentleness and loving care. In an instance of prophetic symbolism, based upon a similar instance in the experience of Ezekiel (Ezek. 37:15-23), the prophet chose two rods, naming one Grace and the other Union (v. 7). The naming of the two rods symbolized the Lord's protective care over his flock and his desire to restore unity among his people.

This arrangement did not work out as the prophet had hoped. In one month he destroyed three of the shepherds who had been exploiting the flock, only to have the flock turn against him (v. 8). In exasperation, he announced that he was abandoning his role as shepherd and leaving the flock to its fate (v. 9). He sealed this decision by breaking the rod named Grace (v. 10). The people further showed their contempt for the shepherd by valuing his services at only thirty pieces of silver (v. 12), elsewhere mentioned as the price of a common slave (see Ex. 21:32). In disgust, the shepherd cast the "lordly" sum into the Temple treasury (v. 13), perhaps meaning to show thereby that the insult intended for him was in reality directed against the Lord. As a concluding sign of alienation, the shepherd broke his rod named Union (v. 14), thus delivering the people over to internal strife and confusion.

Having rejected God's appointed shepherd, the people were

informed that they would fall into the hands of a worthless shepherd who would mutilate them and eat their flesh (vv. 15-16). Even so, God would hold the shepherd responsible for his actions and punish him for his carelessness and neglect (vv. 15-17).

Christians are acquainted with this passage from its application to the rejection and betrayal of Jesus (see Matt. 26:14-16; 27:3-10). Beyond that, however, it has something significant to say about the crisis of leadership in Jerusalem after the Exile. It attributes the oppression from without and the strife from within to Israel's rejection of her God-given leaders. In rejecting them, she had effectively rejected the rule of God in her affairs. One is reminded by this passage of the plaintive cry of Jesus in Matthew 23:37a: "O Jerusalem, Jerusalem, killing the prophets and stoning those who are sent to you!" The people that will not be ruled by God are destined to be ruled by tyrants.

The Second Oracle: The Tribulation and Triumph of God's People (12:1 to 14:21)

This is the final block of material in Zechariah bearing the heading, "The oracle (or burden) of the word of the Lord." The other section bearing this heading includes chapters 9 to 11. The two sections are comparable in length and related in style and contents. The second section describes the trials through which Jerusalem must pass before becoming the Lord's dwelling place and the place of worship for all nations. The oracles in this section also have a decidedly apocalyptic flavor (speaking to the end time).

Jerusalem's Triumph Over Her Foes (12:1-9)

This passage introduces the theme of an all-out attack upon Jerusalem by the combined forces of the heathen nations and the Lord's miraculous intervention to save the city. It is a theme that appears often in the Old Testament. It is found in the Prophets (see Isa. 17:12-14; 29:5-8; Ezek. 38:1 to 39:29; Joel 3:1-3,9-12; Mic. 4:11-13; Zech. 14:1-5,12-15), as well as in the Psalms (see Pss. 46:6,8-10; 48:4-8; 76:1-9).

The intense hatred of the nations toward Zion reminds us that the ideals of the kingdom of God are not the ideals of the nations and never will be. The church will be tolerated in the world only to the extent that it is willing to be conformed to the world. Let the church be true to its nature and mission, and it will always be persecuted. Because strong nations take their strength as a mandate to rule with force and to run roughshod over the rights of men and women, they will never tolerate a church that condemns their pride and lust for power. Instead, they will do everything possible to destroy it. There may be short periods of truce between the world and the church, but there can never be lasting peace.

But let the people of God never lose heart on this account. While kingdoms may rise and fall and their cities be reduced to rubble, the kingdom of God will stand forever. The prophet proclaimed this truth with an unshakable faith. The nations are pictured as gathering around Jerusalem like thirsty men around a wine vat, only to be sent reeling and stumbling like drunken men (v. 2). Or, in a change of metaphor, Jerusalem was pictured as a massive stone, which crushes those who try to lift it and fit it into their own structures (v. 3; see also Isa. 8:14-15; Rom. 9:33; 1 Pet. 2:8).

Consternation will seize the nations assembled before Jerusalem (v. 4). Horses will panic and be stricken with blindness and their riders be driven insane. But in contrast to the consternation of the enemy, the inhabitants of Jerusalem will draw fresh strength from the Lord of hosts, their God (v. 5).

This passage hints at a possible rift between Jerusalem and the rest of Judah (v. 7; see also 14:14). It is possible that Jerusalem had an arrogant attitude towards those living outside its walls. To counter such a spirit, the Lord purposes to deliver Judah before he delivers Jerusalem (v. 7).

When the Lord comes to the aid of his beleaguered people, they are filled with superhuman strength. The feeblest among them become like David, while the restored house of David is invested with divine power and direction (v. 8). The end result will be the destruction of all the nations that participate in the seige of the city (v. 10).

Lamentation for One Who Was Pierced (12:10-14)

Just when Jerusalem is miraculously delivered from her enemies (vv. 7-9), a strange reaction occurs. Instead of joyously celebrating her victory, she is plunged into bitter mourning and lamentation.

The cause for the weeping of the people is said to be the death of one "whom they have pierced" (v. 10). The grief is compared to that of parents mourning the loss of their only child or their firstborn child (v. 10b). It is further compared to "the mourning for Hadadrimmon in the plain of Megiddo" (v. 11). This likely refers to the ritual mourning of the heathen for their dying and rising gods of vegetation (see Ezek. 8:14), or it may refer to the untimely death of Josiah, which took place on the plains of Megiddo (see 2 Chron. 35:25). The monotonous repetition in verses 12-14 heightens the sense of dull remorse. The whole land is plunged into grief, including the rulers, the prophets, the priests, and the rest of the people.

The Hebrew text of verse 10 reads, "when they look on me whom they have pierced." Some take the "me" to be a reference to the Lord. Others identify the one pierced as the rejected shepherd of 11:7-14. Perhaps the one mentioned here stands for all the rejected prophets of Israel, "pierced" by a hardhearted people. The New Testament sees in the pierced figure a parallel to Jesus in his crucifixion (see John 19:34,37).

The Divine Gift of Cleansing (13:1)

The grief over the pierced one is followed by the opening of a fountain for cleansing for the inhabitants of Jerusalem. The cleansing is from sin and uncleanness. This means the removal of all hindrances to fellowship with the Lord. The verse is likely a commentary upon Ezekiel 36:25 and 47:1. This verse has inspired several hymns, including "There is a fountain filled with blood."

The Eradication of Idolatry and False Prophecy from the Land (13:2-6)

Idolatry, false prophecy, and divination are cut off from the land of Judah (v. 2). The rest of the passage focuses upon the cessation of prophecy in the land. Perhaps this is based upon the belief that once the people have been cleansed from sin and corruption they would have no further need of prophets. Or it may reflect Joel's description of the messianic age as a time when the gift of prophecy would be bestowed upon all flesh (see Joel 2:28-30), thus rendering unnecessary a special class of prophets. A third possibility is that it may refer only to a cessation of false prophecy.

Verse 4 suggests that in the time of this passage the prophets were identifiable by the special way in which they dressed (see Mark 1:6). The wounds referred to in verse 6 may have been inflicted by the prophet's father and mother (see v. 3) or by the prophet himself. False prophets often cut themselves as they whipped themselves into a frenzy (see 1 Kings 18:28). The passage speaks of a prophet trying to disown his wounds. When questioned about his scars, he says something like, "Oh, it's nothing! I just got mixed up in a neighborhood brawl" (v. 6b). The rejection of prophecy should remind us that even the most sacred of vocations can be abused. Ministers are in a position where they can either bring greater glory to God or bring dishonor upon his name. Will the ministry be abused and fall into decline because of us?

The Smitten Shepherd and the Purified Remnant (13:7-9)

This passage speaks of the smiting of a shepherd, followed by a time of great tribulation, persecution, and suffering for his flock. Two thirds of the flock would perish and the other third would be tested in the fires of affliction and refined after the manner of silver and gold. When their dross had been consumed, they would be restored to fellowship with God and reestablished as his covenant people.

The shepherd smitten with the sword (v. 7) has sometimes been identified with the foolish shepherd of 11:15-17. In this case the smiting would be viewed as punishment for his negligent attitude toward the task. However, this interpretation ignores the fact that the Lord referred to the smitten shepherd as "my shepherd" and as "the man who stands next to me" (v. 7a). It seems preferable, therefore, to identify the smitten shepherd as the good shepherd of 11:4-14.

But why would the Lord command a sword to smite one who stood next to him? The answer emerges when we compare this passage with the Suffering Servant passages in Isaiah. Twice it is said of the Servant that he was smitten (Isa. 50:6; 53:4), the Hebrew word being the same as that used in verse 7. Furthermore, it is said of the Servant that it was the Lord's will for him to suffer (Isa. 53:10), just as it is stated that the Lord commanded that the sword should smite his shepherd (v. 7). Finally, the Servant suffered vicariously, that through his stripes others might be healed (Isa. 53:5); in similar fashion the smiting of the shepherd led eventually to the correction and purification of the flock (vv. 8-9). It was in this sense that the

Gospel writers understood this passage when they applied it to the redemptive sufferings of Christ (see Matt. 26:31; Mark 14:27).

The Eschatological Battle for Jerusalem (14:1-5)

The prophet returned to the theme of an all-out assault of the nations against Jerusalem and the Lord's miraculous and timely intervention to save the city. The theme first appears in 12:1-9, and these two passages are perhaps to be taken as parallel accounts of the same events.

The battle for the city is described as even fiercer in the second account. The enemies entered the city, divided its spoil among themselves, and carried half of its people into captivity. But just when the city was prostrate and could offer no further resistance, the Lord himself intervened to change the course of events. As he stood upon the Mount of Olives on the eastern side of the city, the mountain was split in half by an earthquake and a valley was opened through the mountain towards the direction of the Jordan valley. Through this valley, the survivors of the beseiged city fled, just as people fled from a similar earthquake in the days of Uzziah. As they left the city, they were met by the Lord himself, who came with his holy angels to complete the deliverance of the city.

The Miraculous Transformation of the City (14:6-11)

The prophet described climatical and geographical changes as taking place in the New Jerusalem. Winter would disappear, and the world would enjoy perpetual springtime (v. 6). There would also be one continuous day, characterized not by the heat of midday nor by the chill of the night, but by the refreshing coolness of a perpetual eventide (v. 7; see also Rev. 21:25). The New Jerusalem would become like the Garden of Eden, from which a great river flowed out to water the earth (see Gen. 2:10-14). Jerusalem's river would flow both east and west, emptying into the Dead Sea on one side and into the Mediterranean on the other. It is at least implied that it will bring new life to the whole land (see also Ezek. 47:1-12; Joel 3:18; Rev. 22:1-2).

According to verse 9, the Lord's reign would be worldwide. There is something exclusive about the religion of the Old Testament. The prophets stated categorically that it was destined to become the universal religion of all humanity. The time would come when all people everywhere would know the name—the *one* name—of Israel's God (see also Isa. 45:22-23). This should warn us against fostering an easy tolerance that regards all religions as equally valid (see Deut. 6:4-5; Eph. 4:4-6).

Further geographical changes were forecast for Judah and Jerusalem in the coming messianic age. The glory of Jerusalem would be enhanced as all the mountains of the land were leveled and the entire landscape became a plain, stretching from Geba in the north to Rimmon in the south (v. 10*a*). This would create a situation in which Jerusalem, situated on Mount Zion, would dominate the scene and would be clearly visible from any spot in the land. Its elevated position will also protect it from any threat of destruction. It would dwell in security, and the curse would be banished forever (v. 11).

A Scourge upon Jerusalem's Enemies (14:12-15)

A dreadful scourge would be visited upon the nations that dared attack Jerusalem. Whenever it struck a man, his flesh would rot even as he stood upon his feet. His eyes would rot in their sockets and his tongue in his mouth. The most dreadful thing about the scourge would be the speed with which it worked. At the sight of it, pandemonium would break out in the enemy camps, as the soldiers began to fight among themselves (v. 13). The people of Jerusalem would take advantage of the confusion to enrich themselves with the spoil of the enemy (v. 14). Even the animals in the camps of the enemy would be stricken with the dread plague (v. 15). It meant a total victory for Jerusalem and a total defeat for the nations.

Worldwide Observance of the Feast of Booths (14:16-19)

Some from among the nations would survive the plague (see vv. 12-15) and would come up to Jerusalem year by year to worship the Lord as King and to keep the feast of booths. This particular feast was suited to worldwide observance for several reasons. (1) It came in the autumn when traveling conditions were suitable. (2) It was primarily a feast of thanksgiving for the harvest, and thus adapted to universal observance. (3) It marked the end of the old year and the beginning of the new year, and it fell just before the time when the autumn rains normally began. (4) It was the occasion when the Lord was celebrated as king. (5) It more than any other feast had come to signify the ingathering of the nations to God.

Those from among the nations who refused to make the annual

pilgrimage to Jerusalem would be punished by having the autumn rains withheld (v. 17). This threat did not apply to Egypt, of course, for it was watered by the Nile and did not depend upon rainfall for its crops. A special plague would be visited upon it if it should refuse to come up to Jerusalem to worship (vv. 18-19).

Holy Horses and Sanctified Cooking Pots (14:20-21)

Horses usually brought hostile warriors whose only intent was to invade Jerusalem, but in the messianic age they would bring pilgrims. The bells on the horses would bear the same lofty inscription as that which adorned the turbans of Aaron and the high priests (see Ex. 28:36-38). The inscription read "Holy to the Lord" and designated that which was assigned exclusively to the service of the Lord.

So great would be the number of pilgrims journeying to Jerusalem that there would be a scarcity of Temple vessels in which to prepare their sacrifices. This problem would be overcome by removing all distinctions between ordinary vessels used in Jerusalem households and sacred vessels dedicated to Temple use. Any cooking pot in Jerusalem would be considered fit for Temple use. Distinctions would no longer be drawn between the sacred and the secular, but every kitchen would be filled with sanctified cooking pots.

When the scarcity of sacred vessels had been overcome, there would be no further necessity for merchants to set up shop in the Temple in order to supply the pilgrims' needs. The word for merchant or trader is "Canaanite," a carryover from the days when the Canaanites, or Phoenicians, made up the bulk of the merchant class (see also Neh. 13:16-18).

We are reminded by this passage of how Jesus cleansed the Temple, driving out those who bought and sold within its sacred precincts, and saying, "Is it not written, 'My house shall be called a house of prayer for all nations?' But you have made it a den of robbers" (Mark 11:17). He shared Zechariah's conviction that in the messianic age no one should bend the worship of God to his or her own personal benefit.

MALACHI

Introduction

The Prophet

Ancient rabbis referred to Malachi as "the seal of the prophets." The Hebrews designated the books from Joshua through 2 Kings (except Ruth) as "Former Prophets" and the books of the major and minor prophets as "Latter Prophets," so that the prophetic canon began with Joshua and ended with Malachi. Joshua begins by stating, "Moses my servant is dead" (Josh. 1:2) and then admonishes Joshua to keep the law of Moses so that it might be well with him (Josh. 1:8). Malachi ends with a similar admonition: "Remember the law of my servant Moses, the statutes and ordinances that I commanded him at Horeb for all Israel" (Mal. 4:4). Malachi not only seals the prophets but also ties them to the law of Moses.

Malachi is a title meaning "my messenger" and probably should not be regarded as the name of the author of this book. His title we know; his name we do not know. *The Targum of Jonathan,* an early Aramaic translation of the prophets identified him as "Ezra the scribe." Other ancient sources identified him as Haggai, Zechariah, Zerubbabel, Nehemiah, or even Mordecai. The Talmudic document *Baba Bathra* (14*b*) attributes the Book of Malachi to "the men of the great synagogue." Jerome, followed later by Calvin, accepted the view that the book was written by Ezra. Nothing is lost by our not knowing who the prophet was. He still remains as "a voice crying in the wilderness, making ready the way of the Lord." Whoever he was, he fully deserved to be called "the messenger of the Lord."

The Style of the Book

Malachi has been called "the Hebrew Socrates." This is due to the fact that much of the book consists of dialogues between God (or his prophet) and the people. First, a charge is made against the people. The people flatly deny the charge. The charge is then validated by incontrovertible evidence of the people's guilt. Examples of such dialogues can be found throughout the book (see 1:2-3,6-7; 2:13-14,17; 3:7-9,13-14).

Date and Background

The most likely date for Malachi would be the period between 460 and 450 BC, just prior to the coming of Ezra and Nehemiah to Jerusalem. In many ways his preaching prepared the way for their reforms.

These were trying years for the inhabitants of Jerusalem. The Temple had been dedicated in 515 BC, but the messianic hopes stirred up by Haggai and Zechariah showed no signs of being fulfilled. Jerusalem continued to be ruled by the iron fist of the Persians. Economic conditions steadily worsened, until desperate Jewish fathers were forced to sell their children into slavery to their richer neighbors (Neh. 5:1-5). Unemployment was widespread, there being "no wage for man or any wage for beast" (Zech. 8:10). On top of this, tribute had to be paid to the Persian governors assigned to Jerusalem and provisions had to be furnished for the soldiers occupying the land (Neh. 5:15). The Temple revenues were so diminished that the Levites left Jerusalem and moved into the surrounding countryside in order to make their living by farming (Neh. 13:10).

Jerusalem's neighbors posed a continuing threat to her well-being. The Samaritans had earlier succeeded in delaying the rebuilding of the Temple (Ezra 4:4-16). This earlier success emboldened them to try to prevent Nehemiah's repairing of the walls of the city (Neh. 4:1-9; 6:1-9). The Edomites had also seized much of the territory of Judah that lay south of Jerusalem, a region that later came to be known as Idumea.

A half-century of such poverty and oppression produced a dangerous reaction among the people. The faith of former days gave way to doubt and skepticism. A new temper took possession of the Hebrew mind, and many began to question God's love (1:2) and his justice (2:17). They openly questioned whether there was any advantage to being religious (3:13-15).

Three developments grew out of this skeptical attitude on the part of the Jews. (1) The Temple was abandoned and its services neglected. Tithes and offerings were withheld. Lame and diseased animals were offered upon the Lord's altar. Vows solemnly made were soon forgotten. The Lord was forced to call for someone to close the Temple doors and quench the altar fires (1:10). (2) The second development was a growing unconcern on the part of the people toward the maintaining of their separate and distinct identity as the people of God. Intermarriage of Jewish men with heathen women was widespread, often preceded by their divorcing their Jewish wives. The sabbath was being desecrated, especially by greedy merchants. The Jews were in dire peril of being absorbed by the heathen cultures around them. (3) A third development was a serious decline in ethical and moral standards in the Jewish community. Unscrupulous moneylenders did not hesitate to seize the children of those who defaulted on their loans (Neh. 5:1-5). Malachi launched an attack against sorcerers, adulterers, those swearing falsely, and those oppressing such helpless persons as hirelings, widows, and orphans (3:5). This list lets us know that reform was badly needed.

The one source of hope for the nation in such trying times was a faithful nucleus of God-fearing persons who regarded the situation with growing alarm. They came together regularly to speak of the Lord's goodness and to lend each other mutual support (3:16). They were the Israel within Israel through whom the great purposes of God would someday be realized.

It fell the lot of Malachi to be the spokesman for this group. Few prophets ever faced a more difficult situation. He lived in one of those uneventful waiting periods in history when God seemed to have forgotten his people. Malachi's task was to explain the delay in the fulfillment of the divine promises and to reestablish confidence in God and in the speedy coming of his Messiah.

Title and Prologue
1:1-5

The theme of the opening section of the book is the ingratitude that Israel had shown toward God. The Book of Malachi makes four significant affirmations about God. (1) He is the God of love (v. 2). (2) He is the God of power (v. 5). (3) He is our Father and Master (v. 6). (4) He does not change (3:6).

If we analyze all our questions about God, they could be reduced by two basic questions: is he able? and Does he care? We would not want to believe in God if he were all-loving and yet powerless to act. Neither would we want to follow God if he were all-powerful but devoid of love and compassion. Malachi affirmed that God is both the God of love (v. 2) and the God of power (v. 5).

The love that God had for Israel was known as election love. To say that he loved Jacob but hated Esau (vv. 2-3) meant that he chose Jacob (and the Israelites) but rejected Esau (and the Edomites). The basis for his choice is not explained. He did not choose Israel because of any merit, for the nation was stubborn and hardhearted (see Deut. 7:6-8; 9:4-5). What surprises us is not that he should have hated Esau but that he should have loved Jacob. Israel's election was rooted in divine love from beginning to end. That was what made her ingratitude all the more inexcusable.

An Irresponsible Priesthood
1:6-14

The priests were the first to be indicted by the prophet. The charge made against them was that they had despised God's name through their disrespectful attitude toward the Temple and its services. The name of God was referred to six times by the prophet, twice in verse 6, three times in verse 11, and once in verse 14. The section begins and ends with an affirmation of the greatness of God's name.

In Hebrew thought, a person's name represented the very essence of his or her being. God's name, therefore, stood for his person, his character, and his attributes. Humanity's highest duty was to hallow or sanctify God's name. The priests above all others should have understood this, but Malachi charged them with having despised God's name (v. 6) by offering upon his altar animals that were blind, sick, and lame (vv. 7-8). To the prophet, that was like serving a dish of rotten food to an honored guest. Let them try offering the same quality of gifts to their governor and see what his response would be (v. 8)!

The situation was so deplorable that the Lord called for someone to close the Temple doors and let the altar fires go out (v. 10). The priests were laboring under the impression that their sacrifices were indispensable to the Lord. They thought that poor sacrifices be- grudgingly given were better than no sacrifices at all. "Not so," said the prophet. "The Lord existed before the Temple. He would continue to exist after it had disappeared. He was in no way dependent upon it. The only worship pleasing to him was that which is the outward expression of an inner commitment."

The prophet made a startling claim in verse 11. In contrast to the polluted sacrifices being offered in Jerusalem, pure sacrifices were brought to the Lord in other lands. Malachi seems to have been saying that what matters most is not the outward act but the intention of the heart. The worship of devout Gentiles, although uninformed by the Law, was more acceptable than the insincere worship of the Jews. This does not mean, of course, that such worshipers need not be taught in the faith or that sincerity of spirit is the sole factor in true religion. Still, with regard to its attitude toward the Gentiles, this is one of the most far-reaching verses in the Bible. It makes even more imperative the missionary outreach of the church.

Perhaps the most serious charge made against the priests in Jerusalem was that they considered their service to God as a weary and irksome responsibility (v. 13). They had lost the sense of the sacredness of their calling. True ministers have always found the service of God to be its own reward. They do not regard it as an ordeal which they must endure but as a grand and glorious privilege which they would not miss for all the world. Our only choice is between love for the ministry and weariness in performing its duties. How tragic it is to see a minister whose love for his work has gone and in its place there is only a heavy mantle of weariness.

Verse 14 speaks to the case of the farmer who promised God a healthy ram from his flock but redeemed his promise with a blemished animal. His sin was all the more serious since votive offerings were not required by the Law but were strictly voluntary.

The only specification in the Law was that they should be male animals without blemish (see Lev. 22:18-25). The action of the farmer calls to mind the sin of Ananias and Sapphira (Acts 5:1-11).

Like Priests, Like People
2:1-17

An Unfaithful Priesthood (2:1-9)

The attack upon a decadent priesthood continued as the prophet charged them with failure to instruct the people in the way of righteousness. Since people did not have Bibles in Malachi's day, they were dependent upon the priests for instruction. Deuteronomy 33:10 affirms that one of the duties of the priests was to "teach Jacob thy ordinances and Israel thy law." According to 2 Chronicles 15:3, it was the ultimate tragedy for Israel to be left "without the true God, and without a teaching priest, and without law."

Because the priests had failed to give glory to God's name, they were threatened with expulsion from the priestly office and with public humiliation, the latter consisting of the smearing of the dung of the sacrificial animals upon their faces (vv. 2-3). No prophet ever spoke harsher words against the priests. At the same time, no prophet ever had higher ideals for the priests.

The prophet's appeal to the priests was based upon the Lord's ancient covenant with the house of Levi (v. 4; see Num. 25:12-13). In the early days of the priesthood, the sons of Levi kept the priestly covenant. It was a covenant based on mutual obligations. The Lord promised to give the priests life and peace; and he kept his promise (v. 5a). The priests were obligated to fear the Lord; and they feared him and stood in awe of his name (v. 5b). It was a perfect covenant perfectly kept.

The priestly ministry that grew out of this commitment to the Lord is described in positive terms. Living in a right relationship to the Lord, they gave true instruction to the people, nothing false or perverse came from their lips (v. 6a). They walked with the Lord, as

Enoch (Gen. 5:22,24) and Noah (Gen. 6:9) are said to have done. As a result of all this, they turned many from the path of iniquity (v. 6b). There could hardly be a more effective program for success in ministry than that. Sound teaching, reinforced by a life of piety and integrity, will produce results in almost any situation. This will succeed where all our promotional gimmicks fail.

Verse 7 is one of the finest verses in Malachi. It sets a high standard for the teaching ministry of the priesthood. First of all, they were to be informed; their lips were to guard knowledge (v. 7a). This meant that their lips were to be a storehouse from which men and women could seek wise counsel and sound instruction. Second, they were to remember that they were messengers of the Lord of hosts, communicating his word and making his will known to the people (v. 7b).

The teaching ministry was an integral part of the responsibility of the priests (see Lev. 10:10-11; Deut. 17:8-12; 2 Kings 17:27-28). Modern ministers are also called to be teachers and messengers of God in a lost and confused world. What a tremendous responsibility this places upon us (see Jas. 3:1). And yet, what a grand and glorious privilege!

The priests of Malachi's day had utterly failed to fulfill their designated mission. They had corrupted the covenant of Levi, had turned aside from the way, and had caused many to stumble through their misguided direction (v. 8). Only eternity can reveal the perverse influence of a minister who has failed to fulfill his ministry.

The punishment of the priests would be swift and sure (v. 9). They would lose the confidence and respect of people and would become despised and abased in their eyes (v. 9a). Something like this has happened in our own time, as ministers are held in contempt by a large segment of the population. The situation will not improve, either, until ministers begin to set their own houses in order and return to the basic concepts of honesty, fidelity, humility, and integrity.

An Unfaithful People (2:10-16)

The adverse effects of the failure of the priests could be seen in the lives of people. A corrupted priesthood had helped to produce a corrupted people. This was especially evident in the realm of marriage and divorce.

Jewish men were divorcing their Jewish wives and remarrying pagan women from the surrounding nations. This was not only an act of treachery against their first wives but also a threat to Israel's very existence as a nation. They were in danger of being absorbed by the heathen nations around them. Malachi reminded them that all Israelites had God as their Father and Creator and so were obligated to treat each other as brothers and sisters (v. 10). Instead, the very opposite had taken place in Judah. The men of Judah had profaned everything that was sacred by marrying women who were devotees of foreign gods (v. 11). A curse should fall upon anyone doing such an abominable thing (v. 12).

Marital problems always affect a person's spiritual life. It is impossible for a man to be on good terms with the Lord if there is constant bickering and tension between him and his wife; and the reverse is also true. The Jews who were marrying pagan women could not understand why the Lord no longer accepted their sacrifices with favor (v. 13).

The reason should have been clear to them. They had not only married idolatrous women but had also dealt treacherously with their Jewish wives, divorcing them and sending them away because they were no longer young and attractive (v. 14). There was no sadder plight in the ancient world than that of the cast-off wife.

Only here in the Old Testament is the word "companion" applied to the relationship of a man to a woman. Elsewhere it is restricted to the relationship of a man to his male companions or friends. This shows the high regard with which Malachi viewed the marriage relationship. A man's wife was his companion and as such she had rights that were not to be violated.

The wife who was being divorced is also described as "your wife by convenant" (v. 14). This meant that God took the marriage vows seriously, although the husband obviously did not. When marriage vows are exchanged, a solemn covenant is established and those breaking them must answer to God.

The translation of verse 15 in the Revised Standard Version obscures its meaning. Space does not permit a detailed explanation of its problems but let me paraphrase it as I think it ought to be interpreted: "Did not God make one man and one woman in the beginning, although he had power to do otherwise? And why did he make but one man and one woman? It was that they might produce godly offspring, a goal that is severely limited whenever divorce takes place." If this interpretation is correct, Malachi was basing his opposition to divorce on the Genesis account of creation. Christ also did this when the Pharisees questioned him on the subject of divorce (see Matt. 19:4-6).

The climactic statement on this subject comes in verse 16: "For I hate divorce, says the Lord the God of Israel." To sum up, what does the passage teach us about divorce? (1) It is the violation of a covenant that has God as its witness. (2) It often involves cruelty and treachery on the part of the marriage partners toward each other. (3) It defeats God's purpose to establish the home as a place where godly children may be reared. (4) For these and other reasons, divorce is wrong, and God hates it. We also should hate it and do all we can to prevent it. At the same time, we should show love and compassion toward those who have experienced divorce, especially those who have been victimized by it. God hates divorce but still loves divorced persons. I'm not sure the same could be said for all of our churches.

The Advent of the God of Judgment
2:17 to 3:5

The Necessity for Judgment (2:17)

The situation Malachi faced made judgment a necessity. The people were wearying God with their speech, accusing him of rewarding evil men and of failing to execute justice (see also 3:13-15). Their question, "Where is the God of justice?" was rhetorical, and the answer they expected was, "Nowhere!" In their view, the Lord either took pleasure in the deeds of wicked men or else was unwilling or unable to do anything about them. Their behavior was like that of their forefathers, who put God to the test at Massah, saying, "Is the Lord among us or not?" (Ex. 17:7).

Preparation for God's Appearing (3:1)

Malachi's response to those who contemptuously asked, "Where is the God of justice?" was that they would find out soon enough. Already a messenger was being sent to prepare the way for his coming (v. 1). The same task is assigned to Elijah in the parallel passage in 4:5-6.

Who was the one called "my messenger" (v. 1) and "Elijah" (4:5)? Some identify him with the prophet since the Hebrew for "my messenger" is *malachi*. Others take it as a prophecy of Nehemiah's return from Babylon in 432 BC (see Neh. 13:6-7). The New Testament interprets the messenger as John the Baptist, who prepared the way for Christ (see Matt. 11:9-10; 17:9-13). Many Jewish scholars, on the other hand, look for a literal return of Elijah, which they believe will take place at the time of the Passover celebration. Orthodox Jewish families place a chair for Elijah at the Passover table and leave a door ajar in the expectation that he might appear.

When the forerunner's work is finished, the Lord himself, also called "the messenger of the covenant" (v. 1b), will come to his Temple. The apparent reason for his coming to the Temple is that he might judge the priests first of all. We are reminded by this verse of the words of warning in 1 Peter 4:17a: "For the time has come for judgment to begin with the household of God."

Judgment as a Process of Refining (3:2-5)

These verses emphasize both the severity of the coming judgment and also its salutary effects. The opening words serve as a warning to any who might regard the Lord's coming as automatically assuring blessing and honor for them (see also Amos 5:18-20). When the Lord comes he will be "like a refiner's fire and like fuller's soap" (v. 2b). This twofold comparison emphasizes the thoroughness with which he will judge his people. Burning like fire and cleansing like lye, he will separate the true from the false, the seeming from the real, the good from the evil.

The priests, the sons of Levi, will be objects of his special attention. He will take his seat bedside the crucible of judgment and refine them until they come forth like precious metal (v. 3). Then their services will be acceptable to the Lord, and the offerings of Judah and Jerusalem will be pleasing as in the days of old (v. 4).

The scope of the judgment is expanded in verse 5 to include the people alongside the priests. The Lord warned that he would be "a swift witness" against evildoers. This meant that he already knew the facts and, therefore, did not need to spend time gathering evidence. Because he was both witness and judge, he would execute judgment without delay. Those singled out for special condemnation included sorcerers, adulterers, those swearing to a lie, those oppressing the defenseless members of society, and those who do not fear God. The last charge sums up all of the others. Malachi saw an inseparable link between personal faith and social justice. Neither had integrity without the other.

Tithes and Offerings
3:6-12

This is perhaps the best-known passage in Malachi and, in many ways, the least understood. For example, even the best commentaries often fail to note that, while the subject of tithes and offerings is prominent in the passage, it is set in the larger context of repentance. What made the withholding of tithes so serious a matter was that it was symptomatic of a more deadly disease, namely, an unwillingness to repent and to return to God. In the total context of the passage, therefore, tithing is to be understood as evidence of the genuineness of one's repentance.

The Lord accused the people of being chronic backsliders: "From the days of your fathers you have turned aside from my statutes and have not kept them" (v. 7a). Let them return to him, and he would return to them. But, totally oblivious to any wrongdoing in their lives, they inquired, "How shall we return [to you]?" It was as if they had said, "Can you furnish us with any evidence that we need to return to you?" It was against the background of their demand for evidence of their wrongdoing that God accused them of robbing him by withholding their tithes and offerings.

When Malachi accused the people of robbing God, he used a verb which means to supplant, to cheat, or to defraud. It is the same verb from which Jacob got his name and was perhaps deliberately used to let the Israelites know that they were no different from their father Jacob, who during the greater part of his life lived by cheating and deceiving. The question, "Will a man rob God?" (KJV) could also be written, "Will a man 'jacob' God?"

It is instructive to examine the accusation made against the Israelites, as it is translated to the Septuagint: "because the tithes and first fruits are with you still." If anyone had asked them why they held back their tithes and offerings, they probably would have responded that it was because times were so hard. It is easy for people to get the idea that they have too much to lose to become good stewards of their material possessions. However, increasing one's wealth by robbing God is hardly worth the cost, for it inevitably leads to greater spiritual poverty.

A curse had fallen upon the whole nation because of the withholding of the tithes and offerings (v. 9). The following verses suggest that the effects of the curse were seen in droughts, locust plagues, and crop failures. The word translated "nation" is a word that ordinarily refers to Gentiles. Whenever Israel is called a "nation," it is usually within the context of judgment and reprimand (see Deut. 32:28; Judg. 2:20; Isa. 1:4; 10:6; Jer. 5:9; 7:28; Ezek. 2:3; Hag. 2:14).

The Lord challenged Israel to bring the whole tithe into the storehouse (see also Lev. 27:30-33; Num. 18:21-28) and to prove his ability and willingness to bless (vv. 10-12). The Old Testament forbids the testing of God by rash or evil deeds to determine whether or not he will punish (see Deut. 6:16; Ps. 106:13; Mal. 3:15). On the other hand, it encourages persons to test God's willingness to bless through their obedience.

The Lord's purpose to bless Israel in response to her obedience is expressed in a bold metaphor. He would open the "windows of heaven" and "pour down" for Israel an unlimited blessing (v. 10). The Hebrews conceived of the "windows of heaven" as openings set in the sky, through which God controlled the supply of water that fell upon the earth (see Gen. 1:7; 7:11; 8:2; 2 Kings 7:2,19). What was promised here was an abundant supply of rain for the farmer who was faithful in his tithing. This was an appropriate reward for tithing since the tithe itself was an acknowledgement of God's ownership of the land.

Not only would God send copious rains, causing the seed to sprout and the crops to grow (see Isa. 55:10), but he would also destroy the devouring locust that might threaten the growing crops (v. 11). Israel's prosperity would be such that all nations would rise up and call her blessed (v. 12). This was a complete reversal of the curse earlier pronounced upon her (v. 9). Through her obedience, she would be transformed into a land of delight (v. 12; see also Isa. 62:4).

The Righteous and the Wicked
3:13 to 4:6

There are many parallels between this final section of Malachi and the earlier section in 2:17 to 3:5. Both are eschatological (speak of the end time) in nature and common features include the arrogant speech of unbelievers, the mission of a forerunner, and the imminent approach of the day of judgment. This section draws a sharp contrast between the character and conduct of the righteous and the wicked and the fate that will befall them on the day of judgment.

The Wicked and Their Words (3:13-15)

Skeptics were voicing strong criticism of God (v. 13; see 2:17). Their charge was that it did not pay to serve him since he actually rewarded evildoers (vv. 14-15). The prophet called such criticism "stout" (v. 13), the same word used in Exodus to describe Pharaoh's hardness of heart (Ex. 7:13,22; 8:15; 9:35). It denotes adamant resistance to the will of God.

The skeptics asked, "What is the good of our keeping his charge or of walking as in mourning before the Lord of hosts?" Their question reveals that their motives were selfish and mercenary. They served God solely because they expected to receive something in return. One of the misconceptions with which Malachi had to deal was the notion that the Lord dispensed rewards and punishment strictly on the basis of merit. His listeners had no place in their system for divine grace or for unselfish service. They actually formulated a new set of "beatitudes" reflecting their faulty theology: "Blessed are the arrogant and godless; Blessed are evildoers, for they shall prosper; Blessed are those who put God to the test, for they shall escape all punishment" (v. 15, author's translation).

The Righteous and Their Words (3:16-18)

While the wicked were slandering God, the righteous were praising him (v. 16). The righteous are pictured as coming together from time to time to discuss the goodness of the Lord and to reassure one another with words of faith and trust. This is perhaps the earliest example of the testimonial meeting of which we have any record.

The righteous were assured that their words had not gone unnoticed. The Lord had heard them; and although he had not acted immediately to answer their prayers and to correct earth's injustices, he had kept a record of their names in his book of remembrance (v. 16b). One day they would be rewarded according to their faithfulness.

The nature of their reward is described in verse 17. They would become the Lord's special possession and would be spared on the day when he judged the earth. "Special possession" is the translation of the Hebrew word which occurs only eight times in the Old Testament. Twice it refers to a king's private treasure (see 1 Chron. 29:3; Eccl. 2:8). The other references are to the people of Israel as the prized possession of the Lord (see Ex. 19:5; Deut. 7:6; 14:2; 26:18; Ps. 135:4). The same word came over by way of the Septuagint into the New Testament, where it describes the body of Christians as the Lord's special possession (see Eph. 1:14; Titus 2:14; 1 Pet. 2:9). No honor could be greater than to belong to a fellowship so precious in the Lord's sight.

This section closes with an assurance that the differences between the righteous and the wicked would become abundantly clear on the day of judgment (v. 18). No longer would skeptics be able to charge that the Lord helped evildoers to prosper (see vv. 14-15).

The Judgment of the Wicked (4:1)

The contrast between the destiny of the righteous and the wicked is brought to a climax in verses 1-3. George Adam Smith referred to this section as "the Apocalypse of this last judgement."

Two eschatological metaphors are introduced to distinguish the righteous from the wicked on the day of judgment. One is the blazing oven which consumes the wicked. The other is the sun of righteousness which beams its healing rays upon the righteous.

The day of judgment is described as a burning oven in which evildoers will be consumed. The Hebrew word for oven is a word still in use in the Middle East to designate the simple clay oven in which bread is baked. Such an oven is constructed by digging a round hole about eighteen inches across, plastering its sides with clay, and then covering it with a dome of clay about two feet high. A fire is made inside the hollow dome, fueled by grass and twigs inserted through an opening near the bottom. It is similar to a modern "kettle oven," except that the flat cakes of bread are stuck to the outside of the oven, where they cook very quickly.

The grass used for fuel burns very quickly and generates intense heat inside the oven (see Matt. 6:30). Malachi had this in mind when he spoke of the fires of judgment consuming the wicked and leaving them "neither root nor branch" (v. 1).

The Healing of the Righteous (4:2-3)

One passes quickly from the searing heat in verse 1 to the gentle rays of the morning sun in verse 2. Here we find ourselves in a pastoral setting where young calves leap and run in the exuberance of being let loose from their stalls (v. 2). Malachi's use of the image of the sun of righteousness rising with healing in its rays may have been influenced by Isaiah 60:1-3, with its description of the glory of God rising to dispel the darkness of sorrow and suffering (see also Ps. 19:4b-6). The concept of the "dayspring" in Luke 1:78 owes its origin to the Septuagint rendering of "sun of righteousness" in verse 2.

Verse 3 points back to verse 1, where the prophet had said that the wicked would be reduced to ashes on the day of judgment. According to verse 3, the righteous would tread down the wicked, as if they were ashes under their feet. This is a grim picture and must not be interpreted literally. Its basic meaning is that when the day of the Lord comes the righteous will triumph over the wicked (see also Ps. 1:1-6).

Concluding Admonition (4:4)

The section known as Prophets in the Hebrew canon includes both the former prophets (Josh., Judg., 1 and 2 Sam., 1 and 2 Kings) and the latter prophets (Isaiah, Jeremiah, Ezekiel, and the Minor Prophets). The presence of Malachi 4:4 ensured that the prophetic canon should end as it had begun, that is, with an exhortation to remember and keep the law of Moses (see Josh. 1:7-8). This meant that law and prophecy were inseparably linked. Law represented the fundamental principles upon which the nation existed; prophecy was the application of these principles to daily living. It was through prophecy that the Law was made effective. The exhortation to remember the law of Moses, therefore, was not a legalistic after-thought, but the expression of a conviction to which all of the prophets would have subscribed.

The Hebrew verb "to remember" carries within it the notion of acting upon what is remembered. "To remember" the law of Moses, therefore, meant to live in accord with its demands. In the Old Testament understanding of the matter, there could be no true remembrance of the Law apart from obedience to the law (see Ex. 20:8; Num. 15:40).

Promise of Elijah's Coming (4:5-6)

If verse 4 looks to the past and enjoins remembrance, verses 5 and 6 look to the future and encourage vigilance. These verses are parallel in thought to 3:1-5, both passages having to do with a messenger sent to prepare the way before the Lord. The new element in verses 5-6 is the identification of the messenger as Elijah the prophet. Elijah was well suited to this role because of his involvement in God's judgment upon the house of Ahab (see 1 Kings 17 to 20) and also because of the record of his having been carried to heaven in a chariot of fire (see 2 Kings 2). The New Testament saw the fulfillment of this prophecy in the ministry of John the Baptist (see Mark 9:11-13; Luke 1:17).

The mission of Elijah is defined as that of turning the hearts of fathers to their children and the hearts of children to their fathers (v. 6). This probably means that Malachi saw hope for his own generation only in a return to the faith of their forefathers. Elijah, who had sought to turn the people of Israel back to God in the distant past (see 1 Kings 18:21,36-39), would undertake a similar mission in the future. If he succeeded, Israel would be saved; if he failed, the land would become anathema, that is, cursed with the curse once reserved for the Canaanites (v. 6b).

It was contrary to Jewish custom to end a book of the Bible with words of judgment and doom. The ancient rabbis, therefore, repeated verse 5 after verse 6, thus giving the book a somewhat happier ending. Similar repetitions are made at the end of the Books of Ecclesiastes, Isaiah, and Lamentations.

The Book of Malachi is appropriate to be placed at the end of the prophetic canon. Ancient rabbis referred to it as "the seal of the prophets." With its announcement of the forerunner, the coming of the Lord with great judgments, and the future blessedness of the righteous, Malachi furnishes a natural bridge between the two Testaments. Its uncompromising demand for social justice, religious purity, and moral integrity challenges us to a deeper commitment to the faith of our fathers.

Bibliography

General Works

Ackroyd, Peter. *Exile and Restoration*. Philadelphia: Westminster Press, 1968.

Henshaw, T. *The Latter Prophets*. London: George Allen & Unwin, Ltd., 1958.

Paterson, John. *The Goodly Fellowship of the Prophets*. New York: Charles Scribner's Sons, 1948.

Snaith, Norman H. *The Jews From Cyrus to Herod*. New York and Nashville: Abingdon Press, n.d.

Vawter, Bruce. *The Conscience of Israel: Pre-exilic Prophets and Prophecy*. New York: Sheed and Ward, Inc., 1961.

Commentaries

Ackroyd, P. R. "Zechariah," *Peake's Commentary on the Bible* rev. London and New York: Thomas Nelson and Sons, Ltd., 1962.

Allen, Leslie C. "The Books of Joel, Obadiah, Jonah and Micah," *The New International Commentary on the Old Testament*. Grand Rapids: Wm. B. Eerdmans, 1976.

Baldwin, Joyce C. "Haggai, Zechariah, Malachi," *Tyndale Old Testament Commentaries*. London: The Tyndale Press, 1972.

Bennett, T. Miles. "Malachi," *The Broadman Commentary*, vol. 7. Nashville: Broadman Press, 1972.

Brockington, L. H. "Malachi," *Peake's Commentary on the Bible* rev. New York and London: Thomas Nelson and Sons, Ltd., 1962.

Denton, Robert C. "The Book of Malachi: Introduction and Exegesis," *The Interpreter's Bible* 6. New York and Nashville: Abingdon Press, 1956.

Gailey, James H. "The Book of Malachi," *The Layman's Bible Commentary* 15. Richmond: John Knox Press, 1962.

Garland, D. David. "Habakkuk," *The Broadman Bible Commentary*, vol. 7. Nashville: Broadman Press, 1972.

Gowan, Donald E. *The Triumph of Faith in Habakkuk*. Atlanta: John Knox Press, 1976.

Kapelrud, Arvid S. *The Message of the Prophet Zephaniah*. Oslo, Norway: Universitetsforlaget, 1975.

Maier, Walter A. *The Book of Nahum*. St. Louis: Concordia Publishing House, 1959.

Mays, James Luther. "Micah," *The Old Testament Library*. Philadelphia: The Westminster Press, 1976.

Scoggin, B. Elmo, "Micah," *The Broadman Commentary*, vol. 7. Nashville: Broadman Press, 1972.

Smith, David A. "Haggai," *The Broadman Commentary*, vol. 7. Nashville: Broadman Press, 1972.

Smith, George Adam. *The Book of the Twelve Prophets* 1, 2. New York and London: Harper and Brothers Publishers, 1928.

Stuhlmueller, Carroll. "Haggai, Zechariah, Malachi," *The Jerome Bible Commentary*. Englewood Cliffs, N.J.: Prentice-Hall, Inc., 1968.

Thomas, D. Winton. "Micah," *Peake's Commentary on the Bible* rev. London and New York: Thomas Nelson and Sons, Ltd., 1962.

Watts, John D. W. "The Books of Joel, Obadiah, Jonah, Nahum, Habakkuk, and Zephaniah," *The Cambridge Bible Commentary*. Cambridge: Cambridge University Press, 1975.

_____. "Zechariah," *The Broadman Bible Commentary*, vol. 7. Nashville: Broadman Press, 1972.

Wolff, Hans Walter. *Micah the Prophet*, trans. Ralph D. Gehrke. Philadelphia: Fortress Press, 1981.